PLEASURES AND PALACES

PLEASURES AND PALACES

By
FRANCES and GERTRUDE WARNER

Essay Index Reprint Series

BOOKS FOR LIBRARIES PRESS
FREEPORT, NEW YORK

LIBRARY OF CONGRESS CATALOG CARD NUMBER:
68-58817

PRINTED IN THE UNITED STATES OF AMERICA

TO

DR. S. B. O.

AND

DR. E. J. O.

WITHOUT WHOM OUR
PLEASURES AND PALACES
WOULD NEVER
HAVE BEEN THE SAME AGAIN

Acknowledgment of permission to reprint certain of these chapters is made to the editors of *The Atlantic Monthly*, *House Beautiful*, and *Harper's Magazine*.

CONTENTS

PLEASURES

'HOW old are you, my dear?' a lady asked a very accurate little girl.

'I'm six,' she answered politely, 'but my *mental* age is eight.'

Reporting the incident afterward, the lady exclaimed, 'Wasn't it perfectly terrible for anyone to let her know that? It has spoiled her pleasure in a normal childhood.'

We may agree that it was perfectly terrible, but not for the reason given. The knowledge that she was two years ahead of the time-table may have spoiled plenty of other things for her; it may have spoiled her lowliness of heart, and, if unduly dwelt upon, it may be in danger of spoiling her charm for little boys of six with a mental age of six. But if we are any judge of conscientious little girls with a mental age of eight, it did not spoil her pleasure.

She was enjoying (however illegally) one of the most reliable pleasures that can ever buoy up the spirits of civilized mankind. The satisfaction of running up a good score is so very potent that good winners learn to suppress any show of elation, for fear somebody will think they are, as an old Irishwoman put it, 'all poofed up with impty pride.' But the driving power of *cum laude* has never been adequately recognized. It keeps up the bounce in human endeavor as nothing else can do. That is one reason why Admiral Sims was able to get such tremendous amounts of good work out of his subordinates at all stages of his career. 'He never let anybody put anything parst him,' said a gunner who had served under him in the days of his target practice exploits. 'But whenever praise was deserved, Sims never hesitated to come down harnsomely with a compliment.' It is among the few invigorating pleasures that can still be enjoyed even in the midst of extreme illness, poverty, old age, and grief: the news that someone whose opinion we care about thinks we have done something uncommonly well.

The only trouble is, when we are asked about our hobbies, we can hardly say that our favorite recreation is the act of receiving compliments. A certain reticence about some of our most healing pleasures is noticeable on the part of most of us when students of 'the new leisure' try to size us up.

A lady who was interested in this subject once invited a scientific investigator to a dinner-party, seated him beside her, and asked him to tell her about his hobbies.

'Oh, yes, my hobbies,' said the lion benevolently, aware that most of the table was listening and that much was expected of him; and he cast about for hobbies.

'I know,' continued his hostess, 'that you don't play golf or contract, but now that your children are all grown up and married, surely you and Helena must have some avocations to pursue.'

'Oh, yes, indeed,' said he heartily, 'we

do!' and he racked his brains some more. If he and his wife had a specialty in their crowded lives, it was the fine art of getting a good time out of nothing, in short order, at nobody's expense. But as he hastily reviewed their offhand doings, he felt that not one of them would exactly satisfy the dinner-party.

What if he should reply rapturously, 'For one thing, we sometimes step out in the evening to the letter-box at the corner, and put in part of our mail. Then we walk around the house to the *other* post-box and put in the *rest* of our mail. We do this as you might visit two horses in a paddock, so that neither of them can feel slighted or underfed.' Even if he should throw in a sketch of scenery and weathers, what a sumptuous form of entertainment this would seem to be.

He could explain that the ritual had started years ago when the children were three-to-ten-year-old little boys and girls. Their house had been loosely built, with a great many choice listening-posts, where a scouting child, found eavesdropping,

4

could always appear to be coming down the stair. There was no chance in that house for a full-toned parental argument without the danger that posterity might overhear. Therefore, whenever he and Helena had a difference to settle or a confidence to exchange, they had strolled out to the post-boxes, always within hail of home in case of tribal uprisings, and there, under the evergreen trees, talked out their inmost thoughts to each other, with nobody more impressionable than Orion to mark their words.

This explanation would rationalize the custom, but would scarcely account for the pleasure they still took in it now that they were alone. Setting forth together in the familiar shadows, after their evening's work, they felt a sense of relaxation and refreshing comfort that he could only describe to himself in a queer word that he had once learned from an old Scotchman. Whenever that Highlander had seen a happy situation, he had used the ancient Scotch term 'couthie' to describe it. 'No!' the Scot had said when asked

about the word, '*couthie* doesna' mean
exactly the opposite of uncouth. It isna'
precisely cozy or friendly or agreeable as
the dictionaries will mostly tell you. It
has no pairfectly accurate translation.
But when you settle your chin i' your
collar and feel yoursel' solid wi' all aboot
you, then and then only are you feeling
couthie.' Perhaps this came near to being
a definition of a certain type of pleasure;
anything, no matter how flat or small or
simple, that can give this homelike feeling
with the world. But it would not be quite
feasible to launch out on any such treatise
at a dinner-party.

Here the hostess, now thoroughly
amused, put in a helpful word.

'Surely you take some exercise,' she
prompted, 'or play some games?'

Games! At this kind cue an inspiration
dawned upon her guest. Only last week
he had noticed some checked gingham
that the Welfare Committee had sent to
his wife to make up into garments. The
pattern had reminded him that Helena
had never learned to play checkers. He

had borrowed a length of the cloth, folded it to scale for a checker-board, used lumps of sugar for one set of men and nuts for the other, and had shown her the 'Laird and Lady' opening moves. Perhaps this would answer for a hobby.

With vast relief he broke his long silence. 'Yes!' he announced triumphantly. 'Sometimes we play checkers!'

On the way home that night, his wife, who had managed with some effort to overhear him down the table, asked him how he happened to think of this noble use of leisure time.

'My dear,' he apologized, 'my mind was a blank except for that plaid gingham, and checkers is a word quite generally understood. If I had gone into a catalogue of the things we really do enjoy, it would have sounded about as exciting as the Harvard Gazette telling how the Commencement procession will form in case of rain!'

True pleasure is difficult to pin down. Except for the great famous relaxations such as golf or travel, the genuine personally selected good time cannot be stated in a word. It needs a complete libretto to go with it. Yet out of our own small idiosyncrasies in dealing with a necessary daily program, and out of sheer repetition of characteristic customs (sometimes affectionately entitled Our Own Little Ways), we can build up a whole class of quiet satisfactions that give us an abiding sense of safety and return.

The pleasures that restore the soul without interrupting its schedule will never be standardized. They come in odd styles and sizes to fit the individual. But if it is true that one great source of supply is the winning of honest approbation, and that another is the creating of homelike traditions, then a third source of pleasure is based on the development of individual gifts and 'gusto.' The only question for the young person is, just *which* of his gifts and gustos.

An authority on mental hygiene once made out a tabulated list of wholesome avocations (including folk-dancing) and

8

submitted it for criticism to the young men and women in his university class. The young men were indulgent, but the girls frankly told him that they did not like his list.

This made the professor more determined than ever to enrich the records of human happiness on the distaff side. So he went around to the women of his acquaintance, and asked us all to tell him the recreations that had proved most valuable to our mental health. The more intrepid spirits complied, with reservations; but two of us asked for time. It was not that we were lacking in amusements, but we happened to know the inhabitants of that particular classroom, and they knew our favorite hobbies altogether too well. When you submit an unmistakable item for class dissection, you really want to be there in person to chaperon your report. The more we thought about it, the more we felt that it would be quite as useful to the professor, and far less trouble to ourselves, if we should look up for him the recreations of notable women in the British 'Who's Who.'

Therefore, we made up a grand list of women, representing contrasted types of character and varied lines of work. We began with Their Ladyships Margot Asquith, Nancy Astor, and Frances Balfour, and continued with Rose Macaulay, May Sinclair, Margaret Bondfield, Frances Forbes-Robertson, the Pankhursts, all the Sidgwicks and all the Sedgwicks, Baroness Grey, Katherine Mayo, Rebecca West, Mrs. Oliphant, E. Barrington, the Princess Bibesco, Viola Meynell, Megan Lloyd-George, V. Sackville-West, and Lady Passfield (Beatrice Webb). We looked them all up, and found to our surprise that not one of them vouchsafed any recreation; and this in face of the fact that Who's Who of Great Britain expects it.

Wondering if this omission could be due to family reticence or pride of place, we looked up the men of these same houses, or, if no Who's Who men were in the family, then men in similar professions or walks in life. And from this equivalent group of parallel gentlemen we jotted down a gorgeous set of diversions, freely announced by them in twos and threes and batches, not counting duplicates, as follows: climbing, rowing, angling, cabinet-making, salmon-fishing in Norway, gramophone, gardening; riding, carpentery, chess, book-collecting, watercolor drawing, town planning, agriculture, swimming, golf, freemasonry, cricket; Asiatic folklore, linguistics, archæology, walking, music, field-natural history, honorary public county work, croquet; sea-bathing, wood-cutting, study of stained-glass windows, canoeing, steeple-chasing, coaching boats, flying, punting, astronomy, literature, photography; metal-working, sailing, stalking, surfing, cycling, singing, serendipity, change of work; horse-breeding, squash, mycology, racing, skating, bowling, curling, foreign languages, racquets; talking and listening, show-jumping, rifle-shooting, rose-growing in Warwickshire, hockey, botany, and investigating haunted houses.

It was a relief to find the gentlemen so forthcoming, but just why were the ladies silent? One can understand that it might be troublesome to profess a hobby categorically in print, because you would have it to live up to ever after. People would send you clippings about it, and advertisements of its tools. Suppose it happened to be curling and bowling, for instance. Every time the public saw you, they would expect you to bowl and curl. But were there no outspoken enthusiasts among the women?

By diligent research we did track down a few. Virginia Woolf likes printing; Katherine Tynan, talking to a good listener, the companionship of dogs, collecting china, and the companionship of her children. Frances, Countess of Warwick, chooses gardening, riding and driving horses, welfare of all animals and birds, reading. The Duchess of Bedford gives natural history, fishing, shooting, radiography. Marion Terry enjoys going to see plays and other actresses and actors; music, flowers, reading, motoring, and driving. Gertrude Jekyll likes gardening, photography, decorative uses of wood, metals, color, etc.; embroidery and allied needlecrafts. Stella Benson likes travel, Maude Royden, bathing and motoring, Elsie Oxenham, folk-dancing and tramps on the downs. But most of the women throughout the volume hold their peace on this item, and Edith Sitwell goes so far as to branch out into a connected statement of negative import: 'in early youth took an intense dislike to simplicity, morris dancing, a sense of humor, and every kind of sport except reviewer-baiting, and has continued these dislikes ever since.'

One strongly suspects that the three Sitwells combined to spoof the public; but even in this family the two men play up with something positive. Sacheverell Sitwell professes model aeroplanes and the bull-ring, and Osbert selects repartee, *tu quoque*, and regretting the Bourbons.

Perhaps the all-responsible Public Schools for the boys of England may have influenced the men to be so much more communicative about their chosen recreations than the women, or indeed, the men of other lands. The German *Wer Ist's* is not half as picturesque with hobbies as the British, though it conscientiously asks everyone to state his 'heart's dearest occupation,' his *Lieblingsbeschäftigung.* The answers are either lacking or conventional for the most part, *reisen, musik,* and *Wanderung in Thur.* The Frenchmen are equally laconic, though they get asked about their recreations with a vengeance: *Etes-vous collectionneur? Quelles sont les sports que vous pratiquez? Quelles sont vos distractions favorites?*

Our favorite distractions! We have need of them just now, for they have power to renew our spirits in transition days. Perhaps our *Lieblingsbeschäftigung* does not happen to be any one of the recognized active diversions; but there are plenty of passive ones that serve us just as well. There is even a renewing sort of pleasure in spare minutes when we simply allow our boats to rock at anchor, letting time and tide wash idly past our prows. It would be a very endearing thing if some fine old mellow celebrity, when asked about his pet hobby, should just sit down and tell us how much he likes to snooze.

In one of the early American primers there was a picture of a big old tired plough-horse standing patiently in the middle of a pasture, with a complete menagerie of little colts, lambs, kids, hens, and puppies all chasing, fighting, and bunting each other in a circle around him. The picture was supposed to teach such truths as these: 'The lamb can play.' 'The hen can run.' 'The dog can jump.' And underneath in bold-faced pica was the legend, 'The horse is kind, but he is old and slow.'

The attitude of that horse in the midst of that enterprising pasture is the attitude in which most of us find ourselves occasionally, nowadays, in the middle of a mixed-up world. We are very lucky, at such moments, if we have some favorite shade-tree of recreation to repair to — some resource or enthusiasm that can

15

restore us — when we feel that we are a back number, that the universe is getting away from us, that our playing, running, and jumping days are over, that the less said about our mental age the better, and that our 'chronological age,' at the very lowest estimate, is ninety-eight.

DABBLING

IT MAY be considered dangerous, but it is always pleasant, to possess a little knowledge. The serious student has always eyed the dabbler with suspicion. The dabbler, however, has more fun. The water is warmer where it laps the pebbles in the sun, and it cannot drown you. Children and dogs, invalids, and strong men washed ashore by storms, congregate about you and throw water. The serious student may stride by without a look to his deeper bath, but with his splendid risk he may sink while you are skipping stones.

Two characteristics mark the dabbler. First, he really dabbles. Second, he talks. A bluffer talks too, but essentially he has something to 'put over'— something he wishes you to buy, or admire, or believe. A dabbler merely wishes to talk to you. He is naïve, eager, not boastful, but merely declaratory — a perfect type of the 'possessed' person.

With one such person about, life is never dull. He dabbles in every fine art and craft which comes his way. He hammers a little copper, and wrings out a pair of iron fire-dogs. He can listen with enthusiasm to the invalid on opsonins, to the educator on tests, to the motorist on free-wheeling, to the physicist on skewed curves and elastic lag. He does not essay to tell any of these experts anything, but his ear is tuned to what they tell him.

There are persons incapable of dabbling. They invariably do well what they consider worth doing at all. That unwholesome proverb has ruined many a good dabbler; for there are many things that are worth doing rather badly.

My pal and I resolved to dabble in at least three subjects each year. Greek is fascinating up to that point where the characters still look like little apple trees and stepladders. At this point we drop it, and assume pastels, for we are neither students nor serious. A dabbler in French may go far, if he is easy of tongue, and wary — and chooses his audience. In the alluring subjects of botany and bird-lore, he confines himself strictly to field study — and he goes not too far afield.

An earnest dabbler never really misleads you. When you bring him for identification one of those countless yellow flowers which look so strangely like the dandelion, he can reply easily, 'Oh, that's one of the hawk-weeds.' He does not elucidate whether it be Cynthia, or wild lettuce, or groundsel, because he does not know. But he will tell you as much as he does know, which an authority sometimes hesitates to do.

'Look,' whispers the dabbler on a country walk. 'A tree sparrow!'

He will point out to you, if the tree sparrow co-operates, that this bird has a single dark spot in the centre of his breast. And this knowledge gives him such acute pleasure that it matters little to him that there are about twenty-five other sparrows over the fence which he knows nothing about.

In regard to the solar system, the dabbler has experienced the thrill of finding a dozen or so of the constellations, and he has looked through a telescope long enough to see the jeweled double star in Cygnus broken up into two stars, one yellow and one gaslight blue. That is enough for him to know, anyway, to prepare his mind for easy reception if any expert should ever wish to tell him more.

One of the most daring and upsetting of subjects with which to trifle is the study of the pipe organ. Here are unlimited possibilities much too tempting for the jester to pass by. Moreover, it looks like the least frivolous of instruments, and grandly guards the dignity of the organist. With this solid instrument before you, and the august composers for it behind you, it is possible to get every delight of the amateur without any of its reproach.

At least three weeks are necessary to get the real feeling in the feet which belongs only to a great organist, but the lingo may be adopted instantly. You can talk at great length about the fact that you are never supposed to look at your feet, and that you find your place by kicking the side of your foot against the three black keys to find *do*. This fact seldom fails to win attention. There is something picturesque about a blind pianist. An organist is always blind in his feet.

There comes a time when simple pedaling gives place in the lesson book to a neat brace of pale half-notes written in three staves. Never was an exercise so simple, so slow, or so deceptive as the first exercise in the Organist's Complete Manual which involves two hands, two feet, and a good gray brain. One hand goes up, and the other goes down; the left foot begins to go up with the right hand, but diverts playfully and begins to go down just at the point where it shifts its responsibility to the right foot. And meanwhile, where is the brain? It is a robust one indeed if it knows where it is.

When my friend first encountered this exercise, he held up both hands and re-

21

garded them for a moment, and then said genially, 'Which one of you is my feet?'

A few exercises of this complicated sort, and you can let your teacher go. If you keep him on, he will teach you counterpoint and give you fugues. And with J. S. Bach before you it is a nice question whether you still are dabbling. One of the easy fugues, peradventure, will not break the spell; for a smattering of this form can be made a great deal of. Its nomenclature is as useful as it is winning. Subjects and counter-subjects, episodes and stretti are things to conjure with in any camp.

If you have never been one to keep time, set a metronome up on the organ, for Bach is one with whom it is good form to keep step. Then it may be said of you that you and Joseph Bonnet play fugues always with a metronome. This is stimulating. It is also the coat of arms of a genuine accredited dabbler; not the use of the metronome, but the instinctive grouping of oneself with

22

Bonnet — a balloon rampant on a green field.

What you really want at this point is a composition in the key of C, with long continued pedal-points for your feet, and a soft tremulous melody for your hands, with slow tempo and refined swells, flavored with vanilla. Play with a Vox Humana stop, in a cold church, without notes, and you have dabbling in its highest form — an art.

Finally, dabblers are the only ones who have an accurate sense of relative values. They should not be likened, as they often are, to the foolish virgins, nor yet to any of the men with the talents. In fact the last thing that a genuine dabbler does — a dabbler upon whom the hand of the Lord has been laid — is to feel guilty before men. He light-heartedly neglects molecules of dust for molecules of truth. He has Diogenes himself on his side, and Savonarola, and Paul the Apostle. He knows that 'every ship is a romantic object, except that we sail in.' So he sails a bit in every one that passes his shore, and then lets it go, romantically. His horizon, therefore, is full of shifting, friendly sails, each made familiar by the slightest glancing touch, but blanched by distance — still white with Romance.

G. C. W.

DELVING

A BORN delver who never does anything but delve might not be pleasant to live with; but a dabbler who suddenly goes on a delving rampage is attractive. He sets about it with the zeal of a professional and the zest of an amateur, and he sometimes accomplishes a surprising amount of work.

Our brother Geoffrey was taken with a delving seizure of this sort at the age of five. His great industry was driving nails. He drove them steadily, and he put them in to stay. He was a rapid workman for his years, and you never knew in which of your wooden possessions at our house you might not find a few large nails securely fixed. One of the places where you did find them was in the back of our mother's old-fashioned cherry bedstead. It was good of Geoffrey to choose the back, but this was because the finished surfaces were, as he explained, 'too slippery.'

25

The last place where Geoffrey drove a nail under his own power and by his own authority was in the wooden seat that used to be slung over the bathtub when our father took a bath. Happening to come upon Geoffrey just as he was polishing off his work on this particular nail, our mother took firm measures. She provided him with a long 'four-by-four' of soft pine, gave him the store-room to work in, bought him a quart of fine substantial nails, and bade him drive them in the four-by-four, and only there. The Scriptures hint somewhere about the sound of the hammer annoying the Lord. If that concept is true, and if the Lord was present in our store-room in those days, then the Lord was annoyed.

The name of this occupation as Geoffrey used it was 'pounding.' The term as employed by Geoffrey's sisters did not need any object: 'Geoffrey pounds' — never mind what. But although the verb was, with us, intransitive, it was in the active voice and it had its conjugations. Geoffrey is pounding, Geoffrey has been pounding, Geoffrey wants to pound, Geoffrey will have been wanting to pound for a long time when Father leaves for the office. Whenever we saw Geoffrey starting off for the store-room, swinging his hammer by its claw as Kreisler swings his violin by its scroll-piece, we knew what to expect. By the time he got through driving his assorted nails into that four-by-four, prying them out, and driving them in again, you could have sold that joist of wood for wormy chestnut.

Unlike many jobs, this job of Geoffrey's had no end. It was what school-teachers call 'elastic seat-work.' Perhaps something of that characteristic is to be found in all true delving. Your authentic delving housekeeper, for instance, never feels that she has finished. She invariably puts her greatest pride and emphasis on those phases of her task that are always needing to be done over.

'I like to keep house,' said a pleasant home-maker to a bride, 'but I don't believe *anybody* ever really *enjoyed* the fell work on the sauce-pans!'

Well, there are times when the born delver really does. Watch her on a camping party if she happens to get hold of a coffee-percolator whose outsides have been left smoky from many fires. If you are subject to seasons of delving yourself, you know how she feels. In the first place, she has the great pleasure of seeing how far she can outshine her predecessors. In the second place, there is the artist's joy in using the fine sand or the Brillo not only to rub the encrusted surface down to hard-pan, but to make the aluminum take on a chromium lustre and gleam like a Manhattan office-building in the sun.

Perhaps it is in housework that delving shows up to best advantage. The thoroughly delvish housekeeper never for a moment, in the language of the elder 'huswifs,' 'lets anything get the *start* of her.' Her natural coat of arms is a skewer and a soft cloth. Some of us remember the days when going to Church was so important a social function that those of us who sat on the side-aisles had our hats trimmed on what the old-time milliners

28

called 'the Congregation side.' There is a Congregation side to housework; but the real delver is always right in the middle of the centre aisle.

Several years ago, when Queen Marie of Rumania and the daughter of England's Prime Minister chanced to visit the United States at almost the same time, each of them, independently, expressed one wish that was not precisely granted. Each of these visitors would have liked to see the inside of a modest American home — one of those attractive little houses that are scattered along the Upland Roads and Buttonwood Driveways of the land. It is too bad that this natural wish was never amply gratified, for it was based on a wise perception that in those moderate homes would be found the most characteristic glimpses of the country's traits. Grand houses are easily seen by distinguished visitors in every land, and so are slums. But there sat all the intermediate little houses in the middle of their gardens — too modest to invite a Queen.

Those who had the entertainment of
the visitors in charge felt that if they
asked permission to visit a little place,
the lady of that house would have it re-
decorated for the occasion and spoil it all.
On the other hand, it seemed hardly wise
to 'raid' a quiet household unexpectedly
at random, for fear the visitation might
happen to come at exactly the wrong time.

This second objection was fair enough,
because the normal course of self-made
housekeeping has its ups and downs, like
other rhythmic arts. Everybody's housework, that is, except the delver's. All
the royal heads of Europe could circle
single file around her premises at any
moment, and, like the gods, 'see everywhere.' They might find the delver hard
at it, of course, but that would be all the
more instructive and edifying to the
Royal Heads.

Nevertheless, if I had been asked for
advice about those visits, I could never
have stopped with simply allowing the
guests to inspect the abode of such a
miracle of perfection. I should have

taken them also to another house I saw one time, the home of a lovely flower-gardener who had just been indulging in a delving spell. In her house, all the unmistakable signs of dabbling would be in view, but, for the moment, in the proper places. The music would be on the rack, not staidly tucked away in the cabinet, nor yet upon the floor. One glance would tell what some member of that household was able to play — Vogt's octave studies for the ten-year-old, and a Sammartini sonata for the 'cellist. The fireplace would be ready with just the right amount of ashes and birch wood and hickory and balsam; and the popcorn popper would be hanging near the tongs. At the sunny window would be perched the sewing-basket, and on the very top of it would be a neat patch basted to the romping part of a pair of rompers, with needle and thread in position, ready for a peaceful moment in the evening when there would be a cozy chance to mend and talk.

Outside the house, the scooter and the

trike would be drawn up in span formation by the doorway; and the family
canoe, just brought up from the river for
the winter, would be sunning itself upside
down in the yard. Out by the garage
would be the pen for the puppy, the
Swiss Family Robinson play-house in the
branches of the apple tree, and a juvenile
concrete mixer at work. And the gardener herself would lead us out along the
pathway to the tulip bed, where the
bulbs would be piled in brown heaps
labeled 'White Queen,' 'Bleu Aimable,'
and 'Clara Butt,' all waiting for her
trowel which she had just been hunting
for when we arrived — this being, as we
have said, her Delving Day.

Oh, by all means! Let us dig like the
delvers now and then, for how the spirits
afterward do sing. In hours of intolerable
dejection and indecision, there is nothing
that tones up the circulation more readily
than to get out something that needs
polishing, and polish it. At the very
lowest terms, we find a hardy satisfaction,
after a season of uncertainty, in absolutely

knowing for a fact that at last we are rubbing *something* the right way.

'Eleven, twelve, see them delve'—the old nursery rhymster seems to have been contented to treat delving largely as a Spectator Sport. All honor to its World Champions, for they do inspire us (by fits and starts) to emulation; and between times it is something just to 'see them.'

F. L. W.

PIPE–ORGAN CAPRICE

EVERY seasoned organist speaks about 'managing' a pipe organ. Nobody speaks of 'managing' a piano or a piccolo. But neither of these instruments has the capacity or the capriciousness of the pipe organ; nor do they present such a fine array of petty errors from which to choose.

To begin with, the manager of a pipe organ has forty white keys and twenty-five black ones on each of four key-boards; a similar number under his swinging feet; a set of white slides, the shape of a domino, representing all gradations of volume; and a dozen red and green ones which make every note on the organ play an octave higher and an octave lower as well as itself. Before essaying to touch a key on an organ, however delicately, the performer must look carefully to his properties and set his stage, to see what he has 'on.' One careless flick of a finger nail on a piston will completely change the scene.

In short, a wrong note is innocuous compared with a wrong stop. It always comes as a surprise when an organist lays tentative hands on a diminished seventh chord, expecting to hear a plaintive suggestion from the back of the church, *vox celeste*, when by inadvertence he has tapped down an ophicleide. Now an ophicleide is a very loud and snappy stop, second only in abruptness to a *tuba mirabilis*. One may not take back the ophicleide. He is history.

Some known errors may be the player's fault; some may be entirely the organ's. Every player of experience has at some time played the wrong note, or the wrong manual, pulled the wrong stop, or forgotten his hymn book, all directly traceable to his own oversight. But more distressing than these, because unpreventable, is the trick an organ sometimes has of 'ciphering' on you.

A violin, when left severely alone, at least will not play. But an organ will. Suddenly, for no reason at all, some pipe will begin, as they say, to 'speak.' If it is a ladylike dulciana or *viole d'orchestre,* one may play loud music and mask the symptoms. But if the open diapason is afflicted, it is possible only to shut off the motor and descend to the Sunday School piano. I have known an organ to cipher through a whole church service and stop suddenly with the benediction like a naughty child.

Anyone also has a right to feel aggrieved when, having set his organ for 'Still, still with thee,' he waits with thrilled soul for his *unda maris,* and upon his surprised eardrums the full organ responds with trumpets and stentorphone, 'Yah — yah — yah!'

There he is, playing it himself, and nothing to blame but an innocent-looking foot-lever which is on, but has failed to light up a green light simply because the bulb has quietly burned out. The most gentle of congregations will hold an organist responsible for such an error; for, if he is not to blame, just say who is. He certainly seems to be in sole charge.

Then the belt may come off the motor

and silence the organ *in toto*. All the B flats may refuse to play, or the A flats may choose to play all the time. A modern organ can be played with a wisp of drapery from a cassock, or by the corner of a cuff. To approach an instrument that speaks whenever its keys are depressed a thirty-second of an inch, one should certainly wear something other than the flowing robe of the A.G.O.

The player of an old-fashioned tracker organ, who had to exert pounds of pressure on his keys — more pressure for more noise — did not have this delicate difficulty to contend with; but we must admit that he was more likely to get a wen on the back of his hand.

A young organist as a rule makes more mistakes than an old one. For instance, an old man would never 'step on his pedals'—a thing that every young organist at one time or another does. The young organist has already shut off the power; why should the organ function in any way? But the wind has not been thoroughly cleaned out of the pipes as yet, and as the minister says impressively, 'Saul took his sword, and fell upon it,' the organist, in slipping quietly from his bench, steps on the pedals, which respond 'Poo — ooh!' somewhat like a very large dying animal. There is nothing to do about it — except to remember all the rest of a lifetime not to do it again.

But even the wary old-timer can be surprised by a new one. It is perfectly possible for a stricken organist to look up from his instrument during the benediction, with his organ light-heartedly set for the Priests' March *fortissimo* to waltz his congregation out of church, and to see his choir standing with hymnals ready for the seven-fold Amen, *pianissimo* — an Amen that has been sung at that point for the last five years. It is too late to find the page; the preacher has already said, 'World without end —' The organist may remember, if the fates are kind, that the Amen is in the key of G, and shake down all his loud preparations in the nick of time to give out to the choir a breath of a chord, æoline, just as a suggestion, and listen with bowed head as the loyal group sing Amen seven times without accompaniment.

Even if he has attended church from babyhood, he can forget whether the invocation precedes or succeeds the doxology; he can completely forget the chords of the 'Gloria'; and he can drop a piece of music on the pedals and spend his time during the prelude kicking it out of the way without success. Sheet music is harmless in comparison to a thick Congregational hymn book, for the hymn book will immediately begin to play the pedals as it lies on them — steadily and in a bass voice. This does not refer to the book on the rack, which is not especially likely to fall off. But a forehanded organist often has an extra hymn book on the bench beside him with the place all found, and, as the Canadians say, he may drop *it*.

When one of the largest organs in the world was dedicated, a few outstanding men played on it for the benefit of the Organists' Guild duly assembled. Every man present could doubtless have played a Bach fugue or two without notes; but only one man present could play them all. The clever little fellow who could, chose one of the difficult ones for his show piece. He proceeded to play it about as well as it could be played, having a great deal in his favor in that he had the most powerful instrument in the world under his fingers. He worked himself and his admiring colleagues to the glorious end, jammed on the full organ — the loudest musical noise in the world at the time — and clutched his last chord in two handfuls. The time-lag necessary to convey to his own ears what he was playing was very short. The chord was not merely a minor to major, or even in the wrong key. It was a totally foreign chord, related in no particular to the composition in question — an unearthly, awful, utterly astounding noise, and at the top of the organ's voice. Instantly every organist in the place began to applaud. They stood on the chairs. They would not stop until the performer began again to repeat every note of the fugue.

Now a Bach fugue, as every organist knows, is about twenty pages long, and contains measures of six inches and over, depending on the publisher. So it was some time before the chord in question was reached for the second time. The goodly fellowship was motionless with anxiety, when their brother, now thoroughly endeared to them, selected his notes with great care, and came down on the right chord, full organ with double growlers on the pedals, *bombarde 32*, and turned his head completely round to smile at them. A great organist can do nothing so absolutely lovable as to make a mistake.

They all make them, and what a pleasure it is to see a really great man heel a pedal that should be toed! But the state of mind of an organist who has just blundered is that of unthinkable depression. He probably cares very little about living to play again. And yet, for this same organist there are frequently moments when, with the golden voice of his contralto above him, the silver voice of his tenor over yonder, and a skillful stopped-diapason and *flute d'amour* beneath his fingers — a shutter closing under his feet at just the right moment to allow his voices to breathe together into perfect silence — he may feel that even hell is worth his while.

He may express whatever has befallen him (always excepting hatred) — exaltation, despair, fear, longing, thanksgiving, hunger, thirst, or the pursuit of happiness. He may break every rule of the classic and add power and yet more power, tapping down diapasons here and there in proportion to his excitement, and horns if he has them, kicking open shutters, stepping on levers, lighting up lights — full organ *zuletzt*, plus tremolo.

For if it is true, and it is, that one can make uncountable mistakes in managing a pipe organ, it is also true that one may do more original and creative things with it than with any other instrument — not even excepting the baton.

G. C. W.

HOUSEHOLD SCENES AND HOW
TO MAKE THEM

A SCENE is a primitive thing. A little child can make one. Its only requisites are a dominant emotion, an instinct for 'good theatre,' and at least one other person on whom to act. A large audience is not necessary; but if the star actor chances to be a competent dramatist, then the more minor characters and standers-aghast there are, the better.

The makers of scenes are of prime importance to the makers of homes. For weal or mischief, they sway the house. Enter one of them in stage-centre mood, and instantly the program undergoes a lightning change. Many persons who complain that community life is turbulent would be astounded if they could see what tranquil pictures their own environments present when they themselves aren't there. 'We did not,' remarked one small boy severely to a sister who had just invaded and agitated a peaceful sand-pile party of the youngest set, 'we did not have *any* of this elegant racket before you came.'

Every human being is potentially either a scene-maker or the cause of scenes in others. Scenes in others are caused by Sphinxes, by Managers, by Pussyfooters, and by Harpers on One String. Scenes are made by Human Firecrackers, by Human Variables, and by demure citizens when unduly goaded or taken by surprise.

Of these types, the Human Variable is the one who will best bear watching. His life reminds one of the delightful term in French mathematics, 'The March of the Variable.' The Frenchman applies this term merely to the plotting of any given variable quantity on a sheet of plotting paper. But translated out of its setting it sounds like the Marseillaise of all the precariously balanced dispositions in the world. The march of the variable has a tremendous effect upon the spirits of any house in which a genuine Human Variable resides. If he comes marching home in high feather, everyone is glad;

44

and, contrariwise, everybody runs to
cover when the family Variable marches
as to war. Such a being is far more potent
to dictate the prevailing state of mind
among his kindred than any of the more
steady-going members of society. One
would be tempted to say that a Variable
ought always to marry a Constant, except that one has known so many happy
marriages in which two Variables marched
their picturesque journey gallantly together, with brilliant children cavorting
in their train. After all, it is only the
high-strung person who can understand
quite how another high-strung person
feels. If two of them can hit it off together at all, they create a drama of
absorbing interest in their home, though
not necessarily a continuous pantomime
of cooing doves.

All those who are Variables or asso-
ciated with Variables do well to study
scene-shifting as a craft. Not only the
drama of disgruntlement but also the
high pageant of sheer loveliness should
be taken into account, and a detailed

analysis might be made of the hundred most delightful and the hundred most irritating Household Scenes. The upshot of the investigation would be a body of doctrine from which each young bridegroom could know exactly what he was doing when he staged too often, for instance, the scene entitled, 'You are a Moron. I am a Sphinx.' Each young bride would learn that it never pays to put on the monologue beginning, 'If you really loved me.' Young mothers of small children would be assured that Heaven looks down in admiration at the home-manager who keeps her temper during the early-morning curtain-raiser called 'Getting Them Off.' And even children could learn that a small boy who has lost his books and 'homework' at such an hour can get a whole family by the ears, especially if he has parents who differ as to how he should be trained. The simplest episodes should be included, for they are the ones that most constantly contribute either to mutual satisfactions or to nerve-fray in the home.

46

As an interested observer, I have a contribution or two that I should like to offer for such a list. The scenes are enacted by sensible busy people who are doing the work of the world without fireworks, avoiding brimstone when they can.

The first is a parlor view disclosing a young man at the piano; near him, a young baritone, singing with all his heart; and at left centre the mother of the baritone, herself a skilled violinist, playing an obbligato for the men. The audience, gathered in the shadows of the music-room, has begged for familiar selections of the kind which artists take care to label, 'by request.' The baritone, spurred by the responsive mood of his listeners, is singing his very best in that exalted passage of Mendelssohn's 'Saint Paul' where the andantino begins, 'But the Lord is mindful of His own'— when the mother of the baritone spies a moth. Casting aside her violin, regardless of Saint Paul, she springs up and goes darting about the room, bringing her hands together with a sharp percussion, peering

47

into them cautiously, darting again, beating her hands again, darting, peering, beating. Her activity is the timely gesture of a discerning housewife, alive to the fate of woollens. But it drives the baritone completely wild.

The brief but spicy mother-and-son scene which follows has for its make-up just one prime ingredient: the Come-Down. Analyze one whole category of the warlike household scene, and you will find that some emotion, conviction, enterprise, ambition, song, or story was in full swing, and a sudden drop befell it. Down tumbled the diminished human spirit; but it landed on its feet with a rapier in its hand.

This kind of scene is far safer between parents and children, brothers and sisters, uncles and nieces, than it is between the two principals in the home. Husbands and wives can rarely afford to take each other down.

Our next contribution is a balcony scene involving an educational expert, his wife who was a garden-lover and woman of affairs, and their eldest son, the adequate representative of them both. The lady of this troupe had been called away on a journey that would keep her out of town over night. Just as she was about to start, she discovered that the Yale lock on the front door was out of order. It was too late to have it mended, so she told her son and husband that when they left the house the next morning, they must take the back door key with them, unless they could manage to get the lock on the front door repaired.

The gentlemen, while she was speaking, gazed at her indulgently with bright eyes. Supposing that they had heard what she had told them, she drove off. Toward evening next day she returned just in time to see her husband in the garden steadying a tall ladder against the house, and her son on the ladder high up at the top of the wistaria vine, preparing to enter the house through a latticed window under the roof. At her surprised exclamation, both men turned toward her with glances of reproach.

'It's a pity,' began her son from his wistaria bower, 'that you couldn't tell us the Yale lock was on the blink.'

'Did you know about it?' inquired her husband with restrained austerity.

'Why, yes,' said she, 'and I told you both about it before I left you last night. Don't you remember?'

Most emphatically they did not. They were not, they said, in the habit of remembering things that never had been told to them; and in this they backed each other up. Both men were graduates of Harvard and quite sure that they were right. But weep not for the lady. She hailed from Bryn Mawr. Point for point, the debate was a very near thing. Harvard deponed that Bryn Mawr had possibly alluded to something about a door, but that she had been talking about the door of the family car. Bryn Mawr inquired whether or not there was a Yale lock on the automobile door. Harvard, standing knee-deep in Darwin tulips, testified that Yale had not been mentioned in his presence, much less its locks, and

50

that if Yale *had* been mentioned, he would certainly have remembered it.

The stopping place in a scene of this kind always has to be arbitrary. The motif, 'I certainly did, you most certainly did not,' has been carried to the Supreme Court and to the field of honor. Knives have been drawn, and blood. Multiplied sufficiently, divorces have been had.

The chief ingredient of this scene is what may be called Defective Mental Acoustics. Persons of the abstracted, creative turn of mind can appear to be listening with eyes fixed keenly upon you; but that is no sure sign that they have heard. There is a world of experience behind the custom of at least one wife who, when she has to convey a message of any importance to her husband, sets it down in typewriting and asks him for a receipt. In almost any meditative household, a neat card catalog of one's more important receipted remarks would be a handy thing to have about the house.

Acoustics and the come-down can stir

up many a rumpus; but they are as
nothing compared with a third explosive,
the Counter-Complex. When one person
in a family has a complex, and somebody
else has an opposing complex, and the
first person's complex hits the second
person's counter-complex squarely across
the bows, what do the psychoanalysts
advise?

A popular headmaster of a preparatory
school was obsessed with a mania for
promptness. Since his control of his
school was absolute, absolute punctuality
prevailed. But in the middle of the winter
term one year he married a beautiful girl
with a mania for the Dramatic Entrance.
He fetched her home to his model campus,
introduced her to his model schedule, and
found that she had an incurable brain-set
that made her arrive everywhere at least
fifteen minutes late.

She could not seem to help it. She
loved to attend his chapel-talks, and
would come gracefully up the middle
aisle in the centre of paragraph five, to
the complete rapture of all the sub-

masters and the boys, but to the intolerable irritation of their chief. It was not so much the fact that the unquestioned captain of the Ship of State was unable to maintain discipline in his own cabin, though that was an aspect that greatly delighted the men. Personally, he knew that his margin of control was generous enough so that he could afford to be openly flouted by his bride. But his life-long emphasis on punctuality was based on a very deep thing: the fine momentum of starting each event with everything shipshape and everybody hoisting sail at the moment set. The sight of one beauteous female straggler forever clambering up belated on to the poop-deck spoiled the day for him. He had been an only son, and a prodigy, and never before had he been gainsaid. Consequently he had whatever complex you do have when nobody ever gainsays you. She had the powerful counter-complex of the reigning belle. Therefore, whenever they were by themselves, on their one topic of dispute, they staged some very cranky scenes.

It is doubtful if there is anything to be done about a scene of this sort except to drop it as quickly as possible and shift the whole of life's emphasis promptly on to something else. Certainly there is no logical end to arguments on such a topic, because the counter-complex may be co-extensive with personality, and personality may be immortal.

The shifting of this scene must necessarily be artificial, because in a state of nature the dispute goes on and on. There is one pleasant home where they have a given signal for the sudden changing of this kind of argumentative scene. The signal was invented by the youngest daughter of the family one afternoon when the whole group had gone out for a ride. Two of the older members of the tribe were arguing hotly, when up from the forest stream beside the road came a little dog, soaking wet, his coat dripping showers of water at every stride, and a spray of watercress clinging to his ear. As the dog stood and shook himself on the bridge, the little girl interrupted the debaters long enough to say wisely, 'I guess that dog's been in the brook.' No attention was paid to her, and the argument raged on. But at every comma and semi-colon, she solemnly repeated her observation, until 'I guess that dog has been in the brook' began to sound as if it had a subtle bearing on the feud. Ever since, when counter-complexes on a threadbare subject have reached a tiresome point, somebody observes, 'I guess *that* dog has been in the brook,' and the meeting automatically adjourns.

Nearly every family that sticks together through the years has known what it was to do more or less of this kind of scene-shifting; and the art of doing it without making matters worse is a problem that calls forth the best talents of all the gods and goddesses of Peace.

There is one household scene, however, which should never be cut short before it has run its course: the scene in which the dominant emotion is disappointment, perplexity, or woe. When one member of the family bursts into the house with tragedy in his heart and a story of his dire fate upon his tongue, then is the time for everybody to rally around and listen. A really good woe-scene has its own wave-length and its own rhythm. It is one of the functions of the well-conditioned roof-tree that it should act as a resonant sounding-board for the deep emotions of any member of the clan. Every person who has a family worthy of the name should be able to rush home with one sure conviction in his soul: 'They may not agree with me; they may not be able to help me; but at least they all will listen to me!' No matter how old we are, it is a great force for sanity to know beyond peradventure that there is one group in a preoccupied world at whose feet we can dump our pack of trouble and have it looked over with wide resourceful eyes. The building up, in a home, of this tradition of confidence and safe conclave is a very precious thing. Homes are not broken up quite so promptly when there is something in them that anybody would hate to smash.

A famous boxing champion once wrote a book entitled, 'Fights I Can't Forget.' Many of us have had them. But those of us who have been blessed with expressive homes have also in mind certain other scenes we can't forget, when desolate moods of ours were comforted, when our pet projects were reinforced and magnified, when our mental difficulties were given a lift by kindred minds, and when, if we belonged to the repressed and speechless type, we were allowed to sit and ache away to ourselves in friendly company.

Not often is it recognized that an episode of heavenly peace can be as intensely remembered as a scene of turmoil and destruction. But it surely can. A lovely home-scene, infinitely enhanced in memory, becomes a safety zone for the adventuring spirit. It may be created from the simplest elements and in the most unpromising hours, as happened in our own early home where the high peak of the day, when we were children, was the moment at which we were normally most inclined to be cross. Everybody knows that fractious hour for children, just at the fag end of the afternoon before it is quite time for their early supper. That low point in a child's day was made into a moment of enchantment by our mother. At every other time she was busy; but when that crotchety hour was about to arrive she would drop everything and sit down by the west window with the youngest in her lap. The other two of us would stand as close as we could get on either side of her, looking out of the window with our elbows on the sill. When there was an early winter sunset, we watched the sunset. When there was a crocus on the lawn, we discoursed upor the crocus. When there was a snow-storm we watched the snow. Once in a while there were stories, and sometimes we played the exciting game of guessing which would be the next to pass the house, a lady or a man.

What was there about that scene that we and our brother should remember it for years? The makings of it were very simple: a rocking chair, a window sill, and a fairway to the sky.

Pleasant scenes are often made of very plain materials; but they are the salvation of any household wherein the 'elegant rackets' of family life are offset by hours of congeniality in a fairly balanced way. The emotional glow of the domestic drama has in it the composite lighting of all its separate scenes — scenes pleasant or unpleasant, but memorable because in the midst of them energies were kindled, imagination ran swift and high, and thoughts took on color of tribal flame. How dramatic a thing is life upon the changeful earth, especially if, somewhere on the crust of the planet, there is a lively household that would miss you if you should vanish altogether from their Scenes.

F. L. W.

SKIP THE CADENZA

THERE is an episode that occurs in music, which even the composer himself will tell you is not necessary to the successful development of a composition, but exists merely as a furbelow or embellishment; — a flourish, as it were, at the end of a capital letter. The violinist, or whatever soloist, interrupts himself at a certain point in his piece, usually on *re*, *sol*, or *te*, as if the mood took him to try out the resources of his instrument and see what he could do if put to it. He bubbles along, trying first one string and then another, laying in an occasional flat chord. If he likes this effect, he proceeds to do a whole sequence of chords in all keys and finally returns to *re* again. After a beautiful hold, during which he tries a turn or two and several species of vibrato, he resumes his piece once more. Now all this is very pretty. It is called a cadenza.

It looks on the printed page, as one old

bandmaster put it, 'pretty slantin'.' When our quintet first assembled as an ensemble, each of us politely tried to do our rightful cadenzas as they appeared. Sometimes a kind composer, when writing a passage of this sort, far out of bounds of the ordinary staff, will also insert a less difficult alternative, located comfortably on the five lines, plainly labeled '*ossia*.' We soon felt that our friends liked better to hear us play the 'ossia.' So our pianist, when running into one of these intricate embroidery patterns of a sudden, has got into the habit of turning to call over her shoulder, 'Skip the cadenza.' In this way we comfortably acknowledge the composer's flourish, but at the same time we feel that if our output is not liked, we will cease to output it.

From the point of view of our public, these omissions are humane. But your skippers of cadenzas will do worse. The phrase is typical of their habit of mind in other things. They will speed up the tempo so that the second violin can catch a train, or slow it down until the ice cream arrives. A 'cellist of this fraternity will play all parts cued in for the double bass, the oboe, and the slide trombone, and say nothing about what he is doing. If the second violin feels that he has played one too many pages of double stops which go dum-dum-dum, he will quietly split them into arpeggios, or play them pizzicato, as if he were a harp.

In short, we play one composition in which our pianist is playing a cued-in harp part, changing in spots to pipe organ; the 'cellist takes the bassoon and the woodwind; the violinist plays the flute and the second violin makes up a nice little alto part as he goes along. The viola alone is playing viola, chiefly because she is too busy trying to read the viola clef to give herself over to much originality.

But there exists for superficial amateurs like us a satisfaction that we know not of. The person who always skips a cadenza misses one pleasure: that of playing the cadenza. Quite by accident our 'cellist hit upon this possibility when, at a public concert, the performing artist did not do any skipping. Suddenly that composition, known to all of us, became all cadenza. It was as dust without it. No use. Our 'cellist, upon whom that particular cadenza would naturally fall, watched with rapt smile as the performer continued his deft clipped bowing as if he were digging eyes out of potatoes. Then he bubbled as cadenza players always do sooner or later. The word bubbling contains the element of something happening involuntarily. The subject cannot help what he does. We find it in a bubbling fountain, the irrepressible laughter of a child, the song of a wren, the bubbles in boiling water and sarsaparilla. Bubbling always looks easy. A musician who is really heavy with skill enjoys releasing some of it in cadenza form.

Our 'cellist determined to have that pleasure. So he gave up golf, country auctions, and gardening, those eaters of time, to study seriously. He also gave up our quiet Monday evening rehearsals, and was completely lost to us. We continued hopefully without him, cuing in his solo parts and dealing them out impartially. In three months he was really playing cadenzas, and in six, he was invited to play a Concerto with the Civic Symphony for accompaniment.

We were all present at this concert in a proud and rather flustered row, quite near the front, and we were really impressed when he struck in with a thrilling and masterly note and began to make the genuine bubbling sound peculiar to cadenzas. Apparently he was as delighted as we were. A really serious musician never gets half the excitement out of being one that the dilettante gets out of playing he is one.

As he approached the final fireworks, he drew a fresh virtuoso bow and achieved a Manner. Back and forth like lightning went his bounding bow, faster and faster, higher and higher, the whole bow flying to a whirling climax — when it unexpectedly shot out of his hand like an arrow and sped half across the stage. The concert master, with much presence of mind, picked up the wayward bow and returned it with great courtesy, handle side to. The conductor politely continued with his orchestra at reduced speed, and our 'cellist, a bit put out, as was only natural, rejoined his support only a few measures late, and finished his performance very creditably in spite of the audible appreciation from the audience.

But when he started to leave the stage, the applause was deafening. For a moment we considered the clapping a trifle overdone, and also the laughter, until we discovered that our friend had left the long end-pin of his 'cello on the platform, firmly rooted in a crack.

By now, we were whole-heartedly on our 'cellist's side, for two such accidents in one concerto were surely not deserved.

'Shall I go backstage and tell him?' shouted the violinist above the din.

'No!' returned the viola, cupping her hands over her mouth. 'He'll see it *when he comes back to BOW*.'

This proved to be the case. He came out of the wings in response to the terrific noise, still carrying his 'cello which he had been too astonished to set down. But when the ovation almost demanded that he pause for a moment on the stage, he let his 'cello slip easily down by his side to rest on its end-pin, and found that the instrument slid downward about ten inches too far. His dawning intelligence was beautiful to watch. After lowering his six-foot eminence to make sure that the pin was really gone, he straightened up and let his eyes travel certainly toward the faithful little pin, still sticking in the floor. He threw out a dazzling smile, crossed the stage, retrieved the end-pin with some dignity, and waved a farewell with it to the now enraptured crowd.

We then fell to wondering whether or not on Monday evening he would return to the fold. Was it more fun to play, even with great vicissitudes, or was it more fun to skip?

To our immense satisfaction, he not only came, but he brought new music. It was exactly suited to our stage of proficiency and our mood, and we reached the second page contentedly before we saw with averted vision that a cadenza was coming — a cadenza entirely divorced from the five lines of any clef one might care to mention, and plainly labeled, "'cello.' It was obvious that even the pianist was uncertain what might occur, for she hurried us, much as the man hurried to paint his barn before the paint gave out. Was our 'cellist really a professional, essentially out of our class, or did he better enjoy our unlawful ways?

And then he apparently saw it coming himself, for he came out strong on a lovely tenor note, held it while he settled comfortably back in his chair, and then improvised a dreamy little 'ossia' without any bubbles or bounding bows.

'*This* time,' he observed with a bright glance as if offering us an entirely novel idea, 'let's *skip* the cadenza.'

G. C. W.

HOME–IN–LAW

HOME–IN–LAW is not only the house you marry into. It can be your own family's house when somebody else marries into that. There is also such a thing as a home-in-law once or twice removed: the home of your brother's family-in-law, or the homes of your favorite cousins-in-law. The only basic qualification is the occasional presence somewhere about the premises of a human being (whether you or somebody else) who has been cordially admitted into the privileges of kinship because of marriage with some member of the clan.

At times of family reunion, these synthetic relationships lend either sparks or sparkle to the hearthfire in any home. Events are enhanced by the presence of fresh observers; old customs play up to an unaccustomed audience; and even the familiar structure of the house itself gains new significance when viewed through allied yet not responsible eyes.

After an Englishman has been entertained for several days at another person's house, he writes to his hostess, not a mere bread-and-butter letter, but what he calls a 'roofer,' in which he expresses his appreciation of the resources he has enjoyed while under that roof. Similarly, we might do well to write a roofer to certain wide old hospitable homes-in-law, where visiting relatives-by-marriage have been generously made to feel at home.

The world would lose something if domestic architecture should ever dwindle to so small a scale that the married children could never come back together in full force to make a visit. For it is on the occasion of such encounters with the various developing branches of the household that one becomes aware of the composite background of inheritance, the interplay of inbred qualities, and the congeniality of selected members of the adjoining generations whose tastes happen to coincide.

When history repeats itself under an old roof-tree, we find out also how a given event can take on new aspects for us when we belong for the moment to the observing, not the performing, group.

A large family was once convening in a home-in-law of the authentic rambling sort. The eldest son, Morrison, Jr., sauntered to the window and observed that his own little boy, Peter, was engaged in dressing the neighbor's cat in a doll's dress belonging to the neighbor's youngest child. The neighbor's child was present, encouraging the good work. 'Now, Jessie Bell,' she was saying to the cat, 'do as Petey tells you, and put your arm right down in the little sleeve.'

Meanwhile, Jessie Bell was protesting violently. She felt decidedly out of her element 'modeling' doll's clothes. She was a lank professional mouser, a born careerist, not by nature at all a dressy cat. Peter was having quite a bit of trouble fastening her gown.

'Girls,' called Morrison softly to his wife and sisters, 'come here and see if this reminds you of anything we used to do.'

They came, and gazed admiringly.

70

They remembered how they too had dressed their own old cat in similar garments, and just how their cat's unwilling waist used to feel when they buttoned him in. They had always liked to sing to their cat on such occasions. Little Peter was singing cheerful songs to Jessie Bell. They recalled, too, how they had once helped some friends of theirs to dress their big white setter in an old red table-cloth, knotting it shawl-wise around his beautiful white neck, and tying its ends securely by the long fringe to his four legs, so that he could not possibly scrape it off. Just as they had added a bonnet to this costume, the outraged dog got away, and ran off to track his master, who had stepped out to be a pall-bearer at a Masonic funeral that afternoon. At this funeral, the white setter, in full regalia of bonnet and red table-cloth, arrived on time.... Little Peter was dressing Jessie Bell in red.

'But what's that other thing that he's putting around her neck for a cape?' asked Morrison's wife Agatha. 'It looks as if he had fastened it to her collar by a little chain.'

'Agatha!' gasped one of her sisters-in-law. 'It's your needlepoint bag!'

The fascinating aspect of the scene was suddenly changed. Agatha had worked all summer on that bag, and it had just been mounted on a beautiful silver frame. Everybody to the rescue, they streamed out of the house in a flying wedge, and bore down on the pretty Sir Joshua tableau of Boy with Cat. The cat saw them coming, and with a well-timed dolphin gesture, she escaped.

'Hi! Jessie!' roared Morrison, clearing the lawn and heading her off from the garden as he ran. Back she darted, in her long red dress, toward the house, over the porch rail, and in at the screen door, which Agatha, hoping to catch her, was holding wide. Through the house streaked Jessie Bell, her flowered cape flying, and up at the open stair.

'Oh, goodness,' panted Agatha as they followed, 'Peter has probably left the attic door wide open!'

He had. That particular attic-in-law was an ideal escape for such as Jessie Bell. Her pursuers got there just in time to see her red skirt disappearing under an old-fashioned low-slung rope bedstead that was stored in the corner of the ell.

'At least,' said Morrison, wiping his brow, 'we know where she *is*.'

'But it must be dusty in that corner,' said one of his sisters, peering underneath. 'She's trying to claw her dress off! She'll scratch the needlepoint bag!'

'Let Petey cweep under there and get her,' suggested the neighbor's child; and Peter stepped forth beaming, more than ready to play Israel Putnam to Jessie's wolf.

'Oh, no, Peter,' said Morrison prudently. 'I'm afraid she'd scratch you. Daddy'll go.'

That old rope bedstead had balanced on top of it, among other things, two old mattresses carefully wrapped in quilts, all the rolls of wall-paper that had ever been left over from papering the house, and at the summit, five storm windows that the neighborhood's handy man had arranged there when he cleaned the attic in early May. One would not have ventured lightly to move that bed. Morrison had taken off his coat and vest and was wriggling his broad frame under, with flattering words, as he went, to Jessie Bell. They all could hear her sputtering and scrambling away from him under the eaves.

'She'll go down into the wall!' cried one of the sisters.

At this, they saw Morrison's protruding ankles give a frog leap forward.

'Got her!' announced Morrison in muffled accents. 'But how in thunder is this bag hitched on?'

'Come on out with her,' suggested Agatha, 'and we can see better to unchain the bag.'

Morrison backed obediently for a foot or two, and unaccountably stopped.

'I find,' said he after several experimental wriggles, 'that I'm caught.'

'*How* are you caught?' asked Agatha. 'You got in there. Can't you get out?'

74

She tried to look beneath, but her husband more than filled the space.

'You know how these rope beds are strung underneath?' inquired Morrison hoarsely. 'Well, one of the ropes has hitched itself into the clasp on the back of my suspenders, and I can't get more than just so *far*.'

'Why don't you take off your suspenders?' asked his sister.

'Take off my suspenders nothing,' replied Morrison in brotherly tones. 'I can't. I tell you I'm mashed completely flat.'

'Would it do any good,' asked Agatha, 'if we all took hold of your feet and helped to shove you back and forth?'

'Try anything,' said Morrison. 'It can't do any harm.'

When you grasp the ankles of a very large man and try to push him to and fro, it suddenly comes over you what an oddly contrived mechanism he is. As well as they could from laughing, Morrison's devoted wife and sisters took hold of him and shoved.

'All we need,' said Morrison cynically after quite a bit of this co-operative exercise, 'is somebody to sing Sea Chanteys and get us into the rhythm.'

Luckily, at this point Morrison's brother-in-law returned to the house, heard the commotion in the attic, ran up to investigate, moved the storm windows, the wall-paper, and the mattresses, untangled Morrison carefully, tilted up the bed, and let him (and Jessie) out.

To those who have had the responsibility of playing hostess to assorted guests-in-law, any such eventful afternoon as this would not appear surprising; for it is well known that such visits are the signal to Fate for what diplomats call 'incidents.' Incidents that never have happened before and never will happen again always happen punctually when a relative-in-law is by. There was one summer place in the Adirondacks, far beyond the range of city water, where, whenever a relative-by-marriage came for the week-end, something always happened to the electric pump. And in a tall apartment house in a great city, when the son of one of the families brought his bride home for a visit, the automatic elevator, for the one and only time in its history, got firmly blocked between two floors, sequestering the young couple until engineers from headquarters could arrive and let them out.

These emergencies are beyond the control of any hostess. The more carefully the occasion is planned for, the more vicissitudes seem likely to center there.

An experienced hostess, about to entertain one of her cousins-in-law, invited her to arrive in time for luncheon, stay until the next day, and bring also her son Jim, who had recently graduated from college. The son consented to go, but, knowing some of the pitfalls that might be in his path when he got there, he gave his mother her marching orders before they started out.

'And now, Mother!' he concluded, after taking account of every other possible contingency. '*Whatever* you do, don't you ask me to say grace at the lunch table for you and Cousin Ellen. Because if you do, I won't.'

'What in the world made you think I'd do such a thing as that?' demanded his mother, readily promising to obey.

But at luncheon, Cousin Ellen looked up at the young son of her cousin-in-law, and said appealingly, 'Jim, won't you ask the blessing?' Whereupon, to his mother's great edification, Jim complied, repeating a brief formula that the boys at his summer camp used to recite together before meals.

Cousin Ellen was much impressed. That evening she was giving one of her famous formal dinners in honor of her guests. The group included other relatives-in-law, and also one of her old school-friends, now President of the Chamber of Commerce, Mr. James Whitaker, and his wife. As the pleasant company was being seated, it occurred to the hostess that it would be a graceful thing to ask the youngest gentleman present to officiate as he had done that noon. So, once more she said to him in her best manner, 'Jim, won't you ask the blessing?'

Everything would have gone well if it had not been for the fact that Mr. James Whitaker, in school-days, had been called Jim. Supposing that his hostess had reverted to the old-time custom, he bowed his head profoundly, and started to say grace at exactly the split second when Jim the younger began to do the same. The two men were well along in two different blessings before either of them knew that the other was on the air — and when it did dawn on them, they had both gathered too much momentum to retreat.

'Why on earth didn't you *stop* when you heard Mr. Whitaker speaking?' asked Jim's mother, after the two-fold Amen.

'Why, *Mother*,' exclaimed Jim, amazed at such a question. 'When I get started, I have to *finish!*'

This would have been quite enough to bring the group together, but there was more to come. Cousin Ellen had brought out for this state dinner all her most prized antiques. The dish for the lima beans, for instance, was a beautiful thing of rare old porcelain, perfectly preserved except for one tiny crack. As the maid was passing it, the dish threatened to slip. One of the gentlemen who appreciated old china reached up hastily to steady it, and the end of it came off in his hand.

If the ice had not been broken already by the blessing, it would certainly have been broken by the lima beans. All went normally again for a few moments, until the fourth gentleman at the party, to whom no accident had as yet occurred, chanced to look down and discovered that he had dropped half of a large red cranberry into the middle of his snowy shirt-bosom, where it was precariously clinging to a stud. The fifth gentleman, noticing his friend's consternation and the gem-like cranberry, threw himself back in his antique chair with such a hearty boom of laughter that the fine old fiddleback gave way beneath him and he disappeared from view. All this at a formal dinner circle made up of substantial pillars of society with nothing more upsetting on the menu than cranberries and lima beans.

The risk of entertaining new-made relatives is conceded to be great. Surely there ought to be some rich reward in brave Valhalla for those hostesses, who, regardless of the hazard, still persevere in making family reunions possible. There is a great deal of highly talented work involved in running a home-in-law that has room in it for the whole of a family line. At one delightful seaside rendez-vous, which was apt to be descended upon of a week-end by nobody knew how many extra souls, the daughter of the household drew up some rules that were gleefully circulated among the sons of the family and their wives. A few of the opening by-laws went something like this:

1. If planning to arrive in groups of three or more than three after the village stores are closed, kindly stop at Wareham or Onset for supplies.
2. All meals served to deep-sea-fishermen before five in the morning or after

eleven at night, ten dollars extra charge.

3. Please do not shave in the bathroom between 7:00 A.M. and 7:30, as there is a long line of others waiting to do the same.

4. Do not complain of
    (a) the moon. God made it.
    (b) your mattress. Nobody knows who made it. If you don't like it, get in with somebody else.

5. Personal religion is not prohibited, but anyone who tries to round up the whole family and take them to Church in a body will be dealt with to the fullest extent of the law.

Personal religion is not prohibited. In fact, it must come in very handy at times to the responsible hostess, during moments when events are happening thick and fast in vivacious homes-in-law whose sheltering hospitality the children-in-law and the children's children-in-law will remember all their lives.

There is one such gathering place where a widely scattered group has come together for several generations: a big old

house at the seashore, constructed on a
modified plan of what the early builders
used to call a 'square-rigger,' with rooms
and rooms inside it, and a resounding
garret on top of it, and a 'Captain's
Lookout' up aloft, where you can watch
the harbor, and see if any little boat
in which you have an interest is sailing
in. The place might have been expressly
designed for relatives-in-law to range in,
and for troops of children to chase through
in games of tag and hide-and-seek. There
are stairs and hatchways in handy corners, so that your chances for vertical
get-away are practically unlimited. And
for horizontal maneuvers, there are more
than the usual number of doors: shade-
porch door, sun-porch door, front-porch
door, side door, back door, stairs doors,
two in the winter kitchen, two in the
summer kitchen, four to the fireplace
room, three to the trophy room, five to
the grapevine room, two through the hall
to the tower room, glass doors, folding
doors, cellar doors, and trap doors. An
industrious relative-in-law once estimated

that there were at least thirty-five avail-
able doors that you might slam behind
you (not counting garage doors or the
gate to the baby-pen) in your flight
from whatever boy might happen to be
'it.' There is also a practical exit for the
agile by way of the porch roof and wis-
teria vine.

Only consider such a house as a setting
for reunion, when all the children who
know its stairs and doors and windows
all by heart, come back there once again,
and everybody sits down in the evening
on the screened porch for a talk together,
waving joss-sticks and watching the Cape
Cod fireflies in the grass.

Yes, for adventures and 'incidents'
and a chance to get acquainted, there is
nothing like a full-rigged home-in-law:
especially one where the relatives-by-
marriage are privileged to join in such
traditional family pleasures as times of
reading aloud by the fireplace on foggy
evenings, swimming excursions on bright
mornings at high tide, sketching trips to
Eel Pond, strawberry picking down in

the garden, chowder and lobster parties in the grove, and, at night, true darkness unbroken by troublesome street lamps, and no sound except the whirring steady whistle of the whippoorwill in the meadow, and the swinging of a distant surf-bell out in the bay.

F. L. W.

APARTMENT ETIQUETTE

IF YOU have always lived in a New England house where there are just twenty-nine steps between the refrigerator and the kitchen table, you will find enough educative material for a Ph.D. by visiting for a week in a New York apartment. When you get back home, it is always possible to pass along Ph.D.'s to all members of the family who are athirst for knowledge, but it is not practical unless you have the same instincts as Lewis and Clark, Miss Florence Nightingale, or Father Marquette. Persons past forty do not *wish* to reduce the number of steps between points. They like a big kitchen, and they like to keep the dish pan at the very end of the back pantry. Therefore, missionaries up that way are uncalled for.

There used to be a funny game on the top shelf of my grandmother's parlor clothespress. A perfectly square box contained just enough perfectly square blocks to fill it — save one block. The trick was to spell words, or something, by moving the blocks into and out of this unoccupied space. That game is the New York apartment to the life. It takes just as resourceful a person to clean an apartment thoroughly from top to toe as to play that block game, but it consumes about one tenth of the time. First you move the baby-carriage out of the small foyer (which at home we would call the top step) and put it in the living-room. This enables us to get the vacuum cleaner out of the coat closet.

Clean the foyer thoroughly (thirty seconds) and, keeping always to the right of the baby-carriage, proceed through the living-room, the other foyer, bedroom (round trip three minutes thirty seconds), return through foyer and living-room, left (two minutes), and replace cleaner and baby-buggy. Total ten minutes. That is against ten days at home.

The kitchenette dish cupboard is an exact parallel, for there is only one way by which every dish can be got in, the vinegar bottle being the king pin. A pile of glass saucers should be put on the top shelf, left, front. Wait just a moment, and if they do not come down at once upon your head, they are in. The last man in is the vinegar bottle, and if you have bought one too many cans of goods, you must stand and hold that bottle in your hand.

After such things as these have been thoroughly learned, it may be said that you have taken your 'prelims.' Your dissertation will be on the eternal question, 'How do you like New York?'

Well, I like it very much. My mouth stays completely open with delight and curiosity, as I find it possible to stop up the sink-drain with a cucumber peel, wash the dishes, put them away, do a small washing and hang it on a rack which pulls up to the ceiling, and take in the ice without stirring off my tall stool.

Just around everybody's corner is a fascinating vegetable store. There is nothing like it at home at the very source of supply. At all seasons we may buy broccoli, endive, succory, chicory, chard, salsify, rutabagas, and artichokes, both French and Jerusalem. And right here, apropos of rare fruits, should be recorded my first failure in apartment etiquette.

Having trained myself for two days to distinguish all the different rattles, bells, and buzzers, I prevailed upon my hostess to take a nap and let me answer whatever buzzed. She agreed, not because she had any great confidence in my executive powers, but because she had a small baby and was quite tired out. When the first thing rattled, I paused, vinegar bottle aloft, and counted off all the possible things rapidly upon my fingers: the telephone, the outside door, the inside door, the electric clock — the dumb waiter. I threw open that cupboard door, put my head in, and said, 'Yes?'

'Lemon pea?' called a sing-song Italian voice ingratiatingly. It was reminiscent of the Italians at home who used to drive around with an old horse, calling, 'Sweeee-et potaa-to! Nice ripe — straw — berry!'

'No, not today!' I called pleasantly. Not that I had ever heard of lemon peas,

89

but then, neither had I ever heard of celeriac.

'Hi! Lemon pea?' insisted the voice a little louder.

Now, I suppose most Connecticut visitors have a hidden fear that New York will not understand them, or they it. And I was so extremely sorry not to understand this ruffian that I varied my response this time with, 'No, I guess not.'

'Hi! Pulla da head in!' yelled the voice. I recognized by the motion of the ropes that the dumb waiter was on its way upward, so I started instantly to 'pulla' my head in. I was none too soon, for directly all our morning purchases hove in sight — Brussels sprouts, sweet potatoes, tapioca, and the soup bone. The least I could do was to take them in quickly and say, 'All right!' with my hostess's easy accent. I knew, however, that the man was not fooled by that.

Later on, having, with a brilliant thought, disposed of the provisions by putting them all on the stove to boil, I asked my hostess the meaning of 'lemon

90

pea.' She and my host made such a wild noise with their combined laughter that they were unable to answer for some minutes.

'Eleven B, darling! The number of the apartment!' said my host, who was also my brother. 'But nobody could expect you to know it. You were smart to go to the dumb waiter at all. I used to go down and open the front door.'

That's the way they were — terribly kind to me. In short, I long to go again. I am sick of taking those twenty-nine steps; while in New York, if you but move the baby-carriage and the vinegar bottle and *keep to the right*, all things are possible.

G. C. W.

MARIONETTES AT LARGE

A MARIONETTE need not come within a thousand miles of keeping up with the marvels of Tony Sarg and the Piccoli, in order to delight a child. For knock-about purposes, he is better if he is merely a provisional phenomenon, impromptu, rakish, ready for a jumpy career of ups and downs, not destined for immortal life.

A marionette of this order can be made offhand. The most unassuming amateur of the pocket-knife and the carpet-tack can get one up in a twinkling. Reduce his dancing elements to their lowest terms, such as half a dozen whittled clothespins loosely jointed together with tape or little loops of wire. Select for his head an expressive potato gifted by nature with a ready-made odd-shaped nose. Hollow out whites for his eyes and centre them brightly with blackheaded pins. Do your best carving on his fine white teeth, and touch up his lips and brown cheeks with plenty of vermilion paint. Pin on some gray wire wool for grizzled hair and beard, dress him in bits of trimming or old velvet and bandana, top off his cap with a wicked rooster's feather stuck on at a slant, and call him anything your young audience likes best, whether brownie or pirate, pixie, wizard, leprechaun, or elf. String him aptly to a pair of forked twigs so that you can tilt him and make him run and wave his hand and bow. Trot him out from behind some bushes, and let him lead a treasure hunt across the lawn.

His stride will be governed by the kind of character he is; and the fact that he does not look too much like anything in particular gives the imagination room to roam. The enchantment of his actions, as distinguished from those of the me-chanical toy, is the manner in which he can use his own judgment about sur-mounting obstacles and dealing with emer-gencies as they arise; whether, for in-stance, to take a flying leap over a butter-cup, or to go stumping piratically around. His charm is that of Lilliput. He is the

93

slightest possible vehicle for drama, and slight he should remain. But he can stir up a great deal of suspense at a children's garden party as he sets off purposefully to find the spot where he feels sure he buried some treasure, hunts about for the signs of cross-bones and five cleft sticks that he left there, finds the place, scuffs the dry leaves aside, and reveals to the five-year-old giants, who are going to do his digging for him, the worn lid of his treasure chest planted in the ground.

Like some of the legendary fallen angels, the stringed marionette lives a life suspended between earth and heaven. He is more than half aerial, less than half terrestrial, and he does not like to walk. A famous master of marionettes was once complimented at a dinner by the statement that none of his marionettes in walking ever forsook the ground. He rose with becoming blushes and disclaimed such extravagant praise, as who should say no man among us is flawless, wholly without sin. Every marionette, given free rein in the matter, would al-

ways walk on air. If every human actor
hopes some day to play Hamlet, so every
marionette aspires to play Ariel and Peter
Pan.

But though the marionette-at-large is
at heart a sprite, he can also become an
amphibian, if you make his head of a
rubber ball, and dress him in bits of
discarded rubber bathing caps. Thus
equipped, he can dive from a sand-pail,
swim to a floating shingle, climb aboard,
sun himself, and then dive in and swim
off again, varying the monotony of his
trudgeon by leaping occasionally like a
trout. He can also go down and walk on
the bottom like William Beebe, if you
weight his feet with lead.

The knock-about marionette will never
run the professional out of business, for
the mere stringing of the full-scale marionette show is as complicated as the set-up
of a Jacquard loom. But for stormy days
when children must stay indoors, or for
tiresome weeks of quarantine, or for
getting acquainted with young visitors to
whom you need a letter of introduction,

the simple marionette theatre that can be strung up at short notice is just the thing.

To a child, the glory and bewitchment of the hand-made stage centres in the curtain. To sit on the floor in front of its long folds; to be allowed to snap on the colored footlights left over from the Christmas tree; to watch the curtain slowly rise, disclosing a marionette stepping across the hearthrug and settling himself down in a chair, is to have the fun of the theatre combined with the miniature charm of a doll's house come to life. The curtain should rise and fall as many times as it will.

If the curtain is so engrossing, what of the marionettes themselves? That depends largely on the frequency of their entrances and exits. Children like to see them hurrying out and in, not necessarily different marionettes each time, though new faces are always welcome, but going as if they had been sent for, and not by any means buckling down to protracted sedentary dialogue. Human actors may have the dialogue. It is not every hero who can leap thrice his length in air when taken by surprise, come down lightly seated, pick himself up uninjured, and go out dancing a hornpipe to music furnished by the audience upon a music box. Let those jump as *can* jump, say the patrons of marionettes. If it is a two-man show, one marionette creeping up behind another marionette is always pleasing. This is the high moment of the French marionette shows in the Gardens. The children in the audience shout warnings to their darling Gaspard — 'Save yourself, Gaspard!' It rarely fails to work.

Halfway through Act One, with an imaginative audience, the sketchiest marionettes take on reality. In a home-grown play not long ago, a green silk frog-footman stepped in from the wings with a paper basket of oyster crackers which he handed across the footlights to the audience. His lines were going to call for something to eat, and any marionette who is about to touch on this topic does well to have a little snack to pass around among

97

his spectators, because the bare mention of food always makes them hungry. The frog did not care for any oyster crackers himself, and could find nothing on the stage that he liked to eat except the candles on the tea-table — tiny birthday-cake pink candles which he said were flavored with wintergreen. So he began to nibble at the tops of those. 'Why!' exclaimed one small boy in the select audience of three. 'How can the frog *see* to *find* the candles, with his eyes in the back of his head?' This in spite of the fact that marionettes are least convincing when they eat.

You can count on your brisk stage entrances, and you can count on your audience's imagination; but beyond that you never can tell beforehand just what phase of your performance your public will like best. I was giving a matinee myself one time to an especially responsive audience, when I happened to remember an order that I had forgotten to put out for the milkman's afternoon trip. So we declared an intermission, and, taking with us an empty pair of cream bottles, we hurried down the long corridor of our cliff-dwelling, found the porch at the top of the fire-escape, and put my note and the cream-bottles neatly in their little wooden stall. Then we ran back to ring up the curtain for Scene Five, Act Three, in which my gray corduroy rhinoceros blows soap bubbles on the stage, while the audience, also equipped with pipes and bowls of suds, blows rival bubbles from the floor. And if the audience, in its pride, reaches in over the footlights to display its best ones, the envious rhinoceros will lumber forward and kick the bubbles of his competitors to pieces, with his flat gray corduroy hoof. The last scene of all is a show given with the marionettes by the children themselves, at the end of which, of course, the marionette actors lie dead among their strings, as often happens to real actors when the public has besieged the dressing-rooms after the curtain calls.

I gathered that the afternoon was deemed a great success. But later I learned that the mother of my guests had asked them that evening what I had found to amuse them. 'Oh, Mother!' cried the youngest. 'We had the Most Fun! *She took us down the hall to look at the Milk Bottles!*'

Perhaps some day a resourceful puppet-smith will think to make a tiny marion-ette milk-bottle with ruffled paper cap, running after the milk-man's horse and wagon; and when that happens, not even Tony Sarg's marionette oysters, who walk around after the Walrus and the Car-penter, will be able to rival him.

Children are mysterious, and so are marionettes. Puppets with strings are the most metaphorical playthings in the world. They are almost too eerie to be exactly toys. 'You can not,' said one tiny boy, 'take them to bed with you and huddle them.' The true marionette refuses to be huddled in any way. When he is in ac-tion, not even a fellow marionette dares to come too near his maze of strings. It was not for nothing that, at Christmas time, a busy marionette maker once exclaimed, when her husband found her at work and suddenly bent to kiss her, 'Look out! Oh, dearest, be careful! You'll tangle up your *strings!*'

It is just as well not to work too long at a time with the creatures, for there is a trace of the diabolical about them. They make you see strings everywhere. Go out in the evening, after a session with them, and the world itself seems pendent, and all its inhabitants high-strung. Marionette automobiles go skimming by, avoiding each other by a string's breadth. Puppet policemen wig-wag at the corners, obedient to the jerk of the traffic-lights. The city stands behind all this like an enchanted back-drop; earthly plans are only such things as dreams depend on; and, up above, a marionette half-moon hangs, just a bit lop-sided, in the sky.

F. L. W.

HAY FEVER: AN INTERRUPTION

THREE sneezes are lucky; nineteen are unlucky. One sneeze, isolated, can be taken as proof that you have not the authentic, aristocratic, Henry Ward Beecher variety of hay fever.

Hay fever arrives and combusts on the minute. Every sufferer tries to forget his particular date, only confiding to other sufferers what date he is trying to forget. Nevertheless, his day, like the Fourth of July, is invariably announced in the early morning twilight by an explosion. If you forget Independence Day, or your rendezvous with the hay fever, the explosion occurs just the same.

Few things, indeed, seem to have any effect on the Hay. Sprays and sprayers, tubes of this, tubes of that, cooking soda, drinking with meals, drinking between meals, no drinking, no meals, no meat, no sugar, salves and precious ointments — these have no influence. Hay fever sometimes thrives on ragweed serum, much as mice seem to fatten on Rat-Snap. It remains, therefore, for a victim to acquire by degrees a hay-fever-trained family, and to continue sneezing in his own favorite way.

It would seem simple to continue to sneeze; but until the family is trained, even this may be attended by a difficulty. Contrary to popular notion, the actual sneeze, per se, is not the most disagreeable part of hay fever. The intolerable phase is that curious sensation of things impending, which immediately precedes a sneeze. If this sensation is not brought to a victorious conclusion, it leaves its medium suspended in air, thwarted, irascible.

One sneeze, according to the Hay Fever Manual, is normally followed by another. One bright glance at the sufferer is usually sufficient to ascertain whether he has reached the end of his progression, or whether he stands ready, by the book, still waiting accomplishment. A chance question aimed at him just at this crucial moment is absolutely certain to frustrate the sneeze. This makes him ugly.

I have explained all this carefully to my family, in words of one syllable. 'When I shall have sneezed once,' I tell them impressively, 'wait and see if I shall sneeze again.' They assent understandingly, and when the proper moment arrives, they, with mob pyschology, obey.

There has occurred one famous exception, in the case of a recalcitrant sister, whose sympathy is adequate, but whose passion for conversation is at all times equal to my own. Certain members of the family were getting ready for church on Sunday morning. For two weeks now, I myself had eschewed Divine Worship. I do not care for crying, and my hay looked a good deal like it. Cousin Mary, therefore, kindly took my Sunday School class, unless she, in turn, sublet it to Cousin Ruth. Our conversation savored of quiet speculation as to who my substitute would be, when the telephone interrupted. I answered, for I was still active, and able, at times, to talk. The family listened with interest to my enlightening though one-sided conversation. At the close of the episode, our lines ran thus:

'Mary will take it,' I said briefly, prevented from further speech by an astounding sneeze.

'Mary who?' inquired Sister pleasantly, from the next room.

Prolonged pause, heavy with silence.

'Mary *who?*' repeated the Voice.

Still longer pause, heavier than ever.

Sister came out to investigate this unconventionality, and visualized all too late the closed eyes, puckered brow, and open mouth, known instantly to the semitrained as precursor of trouble. But no trouble arrived.

'Mary Pickford,' said I, bitterly, shutting my mouth, defeated.

'Mary Magdalen,' remarked a sympathizer from another room.

'Mary Lyon,' said Father placidly, putting on his hat.

Stricken with remorse, the offender made her way to a dark clothes-closet, and went in and shut the door. From within we could hear stifled sounds of repentance, smothered hysteria, and such probable Marys as occurred to her mind at the moment — Mary E. Wilkins, Bloody Mary, Mary Elizabeth, Mary Chilton, Mary, Mary, Quite Contrary, and Mary, Queen of Scots. No sneeze has since been spoiled for me by relatives.

But hay fever (I hesitate to generalize), *my* hay fever, is vulnerable in one spot. This was discovered by accident one day, when the house started to burn down. After the fire had been successfully dealt with, we realized that the hay had vanished. When we spoke its name, it returned. We then began to test all forms of excitement. Tragedy was found to work most effectually, then Accident, then Crime. I shall have to acknowledge that all my life I have been carefully led out of range of all horses taken in a fit, all line-men climbing their poles, all highwaymen and runaway motor-cycles pursuing their callings. These are now pointed out to me in hay fever season, with all details noted; for shock has been found to succeed where cocaine fails. It is more difficult than you would think, to keep yourself constantly

in the way of perils: in perils of robbers,
in perils of the sea, in perils of your own
countrymen. We then found that Com-
edy, mixed with uncertainty and a trifle
of apprehension, sometimes gives a moment of relief.

My brother's friend, a man of conventional habits, once visited us when au-
tumn vegetation was at its height. He
is as resourceful as he is correct, and he
saw at once that he had it in his power to
alleviate my hay. He has a faculty of
standing on his head. He can remain in
this position indefinitely. He will do this
for my brother, for my brother's other
friend, and for my brother's other friend's
dog. He will also do it for me. I hope
that it is unnecessary to state that I
should never have thought of requesting
it. But the gratuitous sight of the un-
steady wavering of two pepper-and-salt
legs gave me a complete respite. He pur-
posely wavered in my general direction,
like a half-chopped tree, which, by every
law of physics, would fall, if it fell, on me.

But I could not keep my brother's best

friend perpetually on his head, although he was perfectly willing to serve me in this way. I knew that I ought to go to the mountains, but I wanted to go to the sea. When one likes each detail connected with the sea — fog, fog-horns, sand, sand-fleas, sun, sun-burn — it is a tragic story to turn one's back and head for the hills. I remembered one beach where I was certain there was no vegetation; a few spears of beach-grass, perhaps; an aged little evergreen growing solidly in sand; but, aside from that, nothing but purple water, gray sails, and clear wind. It seemed pessimistic to believe that salt wind, piping over the Atlantic straight from Madeira, could be laden with pollen.

I resolved to sit upon sand, as near Madeira as possible. But, as we followed the porter up the steps of the little Inn, we saw for the first time the giant rag-weed, growing in the cracks of solid masonry, waving its tails.

'I think I had better go to the mountains,' said I, unable to close my mouth after any of these words.

HAY FEVER: AN INTERRUPTION

We sat on the rocks for the afternoon, to bid farewell to the wheeling gulls and the fine blue line that marked off Madeira. Down by the water's edge, there appeared a rat, about the size of a collie puppy, and apparently enjoying the same games. We are not afraid of rats, but they attract our attention. This rat dispelled the hay fever. He made little runs in our direction, scuttling enough of the time out of sight to provide the necessary uncertainty. At last he headed for our feet, galloping like a rocking-horse over the stones.

'Go home! Go HOME!' I shouted, judging him to be an American rat. He was, apparently, for he veered sharply on one wheel and disappeared under the rocks. After a pause, I sneezed seven times.

'Perhaps he is under the rocks we are sitting on,' suggested my companion.

I stopped sneezing, clearly entertained. We added Rats to our list.

Theories about hay fever are amusing and ingenious, and their name is Legion. Hay fever is a disease of the nerves, a disease of the nose, a disease of the metabolism. It is brought to New England from the Western prairies by a remarkable wind, unnamed. It is caused by heat, light, exertion, anæmia, and the absence of eczema; that is, if you have eczema, it means that if you did not have eczema, you would be having hay fever. Some people even like, for variety, to change about — eczema one year and hay fever the next.

However, all wits agree that hay fever is a great bore, and can be cured by neither fasting nor prayer. You must go to the mountains — even unto Bethlehem. And even there, it may be argued that, although you do not sneeze, you are still in a *state* of hay fever. This condition is comparable to a state of war — insecure and ominous, albeit uneventful.

A genuine sufferer, however, largely prefers a state to a paroxysm, caring very little, in his unbadgered moments, whether his infirmity is an acidosis, a protein, or a state of mind.

G. C. W.

THE GOOD USE OF WORRY

IT IS always a pleasure to remember occasions when we have worried to some purpose; occasions when, because we were irrationally worried, we took all sorts of fantastic precautions, which turned out later to be the only things that saved the day.

We are constantly told not to cross bridges before we come to them. That is all very well for the prosperous singleton who skips through life without having to lend a hand to those behind him or ahead. But the general of an army, who knows he must maneuver his troops over a flooded river in the distance, does well to gallop down ahead of time and indulge in a dress rehearsal, to see if the bridge is there, substantial and adequately guarded, before he marches his men down the water-shed and orders them across. There are few satisfactions equal to being at the mercy of a leader who knows how to worry madly, who

starts his worrying long beforehand —
who hates it so much that he can be
trusted to invent enough emergency de-
vices to keep the disasters that he im-
agines so vividly from coming to pass.

Worry can be a disease, a mannerism,
a social nuisance, or a useful art. We can
let it whirl us into an insane asylum, or
we can let it wind us up precisely to the
point at which we make our most original
discoveries and do our most ambitious
work.

The person with a natural bent for
worry finds it almost impossible, anyway,
to keep from doing it at times. If he tries
too hard not to worry, he begins to worry
lest he worry. He has gained nothing by
this exchange, except a wheel within a
wheel, the most insidious form of worry
in the world. What he needs is a zoning
law for worry, and some slight encourage-
ment in the technology of putting it to
use.

In the first place, as to topics. Six of
the great zones of subject-matter are
these:

THE GOOD USE OF WORRY

The Worry of Ways and Means
The Worry of the Mysterious Summons
Vicarious Worry
Nebulous Worry about the Inconsequential
The Worry of the Inevitable
The Worry of the Irrevocable

To illustrate the simplest use of worry, suppose we are worrying about ways and means, and suppose we have cause to, and there seems to be no way out. At least, as one scientific expert remarked of his problem, "The exit is by no means conspicuous." Around and around our worry goes upon its beaten track, which differs from an actual race-course only because it has no umpire's tape to mark the goal. Our worry makes the circuit only to repeat, bringing the same topic back again over and over before the mind's eye. It is an eerie thing to contemplate at dead of night.

This kind of worry, rightly studied, can be the inspiration of strategy, ingenuity, and good design. Around and around the worry goes. If we gaze at it aghast or try to look the other way until we are confused and dizzy, it does us only harm. But if we observe it with alert discrimination, we get ideas. If we have worried thoroughly enough, we have observed in our mind's eye all the outlandish accidents, calamities, and insidious treacheries that are inherent in the situation, and we can shrewdly proceed against them. Cool, calculated foresight at our desk with pencil and paper would have suggested a good many of these, but not with such vividness and flash, and not with such a horrifying sense of the details of their reality. The careful engineer trusts his 'paper-work' up to a certain point, but before he hands his product over to the public, he likes to see his actual chassis go out to the proving-track, and there, under far worse than probable actual conditions, go spinning at top speed endlessly around and around. The detached, tranquil state of mind thinks only of reasonable contingencies. Worry, being essentially unreasonable, reveals unreasonable things. In actual practice, things that happen are often completely unreasonable. Therefore, if we pay keen attention to those illogical states of panicky prognostication which we call worry, we are often usefully forewarned. We are goaded into making provisions which head off outlandish accidents, in a way that makes the onlookers, who observe the hair's-breadth outcome, call it our good luck.

This race-track use of worry for analysis, revelation, and invention is a purely personal thing, although it often brings results that those affected by our actions could not afford to miss. But the second use of worry is much broader, and has social applications that are far-reaching in their effects.

We shall understand it best if we study it in its most primitive phase, in connection with the Mysterious Summons, the first form of worry, and the last one, to assail the human soul.

'Harry, you may come to my desk,' said the teacher. And, later on, at home, Harry reported his adventure thus: 'She called me to her desk, and I suppose I looked worried, for she said, "It's all right, Harry. I only wanted you to take this note for me to the janitor." And as soon as she said that, I let my toes out.'

'You *what?*' inquired his mother.

'I let my toes out,' he repeated. 'Don't you know how you tuck up your toes inside your shoes when you don't know what's coming? As soon as she told me what she wanted, I let my toes out.'

Now, to the right-living human spirit, the Mysterious Summons is far more impressive than it is to the criminal class. I do not mean necessarily the Angel of Death, or even the Warrant from the Sheriff, or the verdict of the jury. I mean all sorts of sudden callings to account, including conferences with partners and employers, official investigations, arraignments by gossip, and interviews with one's own soul. No efforts are too arduous, no achievements too costly, if they will win the right to look one's own associates and one's own Inquiring Conscience in the eye.

Once upon a time, twenty of the most influential students on a college campus

116

received in their mail-boxes certain little notes that bade them appear at the Dean's office the next day. Not one of the twenty knew that the other nineteen had received the summons too. If they had been able to confide this fact in one another, their anxieties would have vanished, because the list included the chief seers and apostles and stars in various activities of the campus generation at that time. But a note from the Dean's office is not a thing you advertise— not if you are an apostle. Therefore twenty students spent an introspective night.

They had no cause to worry; but even if your record is excellent you may not be conceited enough to relish being hauled up before the Dean. Even so, there was no need of worrying quite so hard. The High Authority in that college was not a mediæval executioner, and there were many campus miscreants who spent most of their time between classes going in and out of the Dean's office in a sort of basket weave. The point was that each of those twenty selected students was far better

117

at the art of worrying than the deepest-dyed campus miscreant who ever lived. If the habitual miscreant possessed half that inventive power to worry, he would not habitually miscreate. He would hate the mental consequences too much, for they are, in a thoroughly responsible character, very dire. Those students lived till morning, barely, and at the opening of the Dean's office they convened, each brightening perceptibly as each of the others came to view. The Dean hailed them with hearty cordiality, invited them into his office, and asked them if they would be willing to serve on a Faculty-Student Board to revise the schedule of classes for the Honor Students in the coming year.

This story, at first glance, might be taken as an illustration of the foolishness of worry. But it also reveals how instantaneously the full-blooded racer pricks up and snuffs the air at the slightest rattle of the whip-stock in the socket. Because of the very fact that worry is such a torment to the highly-organized spirit, the greatest experts at it become on that very account expert in other fields. They abhor worry too much to risk it lightly. Galsworthy worried about his writing, and toiled eternally to improve. Forbes-Robertson worried about his acting. Abraham Lincoln was a deeply furrowed and worried man. The individuals who accomplish the most distinguished feats, put things through with flying colors, and glorify every relationship they enter into, are the very ones who would most infallibly worry their heads off if even their own consciences told them that their work was slack. Worry serves the same purpose in the world of human relations that pain serves in the physical realm: it is a warning, and a preventive. For certain prime reasons, such as the glory of a large family, one will risk great worry — just as, for the same reason, one will risk great pain. But the well-tempered soul will not risk either pain or worry for himself or others without good reason. This protects both the individual and society. Those who are rightly sensi-

tive to the acute and instructive pangs
of worry do not run about, spiritually
speaking, setting fires or throwing knives.

This leads directly to a third very
powerful use of worry which should be
resorted to only in desperate emergencies:
the use of worry as a threat. An unfair
degree of control has often been exercised
by the plaintive words, 'Please don't do
so-and-so, or I shall worry night and day.'
This is all but equivalent to the threat of
tears, and has moved many a stout heart
to cautious, or secretive, ways. The careless use of this weapon is nothing short of
vicious. Yet there is one point here at
which worry has undoubtedly served an
important racial use. Many an impet-
uous spirit has been able to refrain from
folly because he knew into what depths
of Vicarious Worry any hare-brained deed
of his would plunge the family at home.

The chivalrous act of refusing to cause
unnecessary uneasiness in others is a
health-preserving element in human affairs. It is only when the menace of vicarious worry is used as a bludgeon that

it becomes malicious. Enormous self-control is required to refrain from using such a handy tool, when it would save one infinite mental wear and tear. A courageous mother, noted for never thwarting her inventive family, once remarked, 'I try not to worry about my grown-up children, but I can't help holding my breath sometimes and *sitting forward*.' To have good cause for worry, and still to let the brave adventurer fly free — that is the nobility of soul that animates an Eleanor Bolling or a Marie Byrd. One of the most comradely lines ever printed is found on the fly-leaf of 'I Like Diving,' where Tom Eadie, the deep sea diver, dedicates his book, 'To my wife, who worries about me.'

A consolidating fact in a changeful world, the knowledge that there is somebody whose capacity for Vicarious Worry we can at any time enlist in our behalf.

'Do you mean to tell me,' asked a sympathetic wife of her husband, 'do you mean to tell me that you have *forgotten* what you were so anxious about last week?

And I absolutely broke my heart for you at the time!'

'It's true,' he admitted, 'that I've forgotten what it was that was bothering me so. But I *do* remember how nicely your heart broke!'

Even the hardened criminal who has killed off all his wives and relatives feels badly-treated by Fate and very much disheartened when he suddenly realizes that there is nobody left on earth to care if he should come to grief. To know that one's ups and downs mean much to somebody else is emotionally a steadying thought.

The only totally useless form of worry is the Nebulous and Inconsequential. It should be taken straight to the medical profession for advice. Its vague and morbid brooding serves no valuable purpose, except perhaps as a danger-signal about the general health.

This, however, must not be confounded with the two final disciplinary zones of worry, the Worry of the Inevitable, and the Worry of the Irrevocable. These can never be dismissed from the full scale of emotion's range. There they are. They are the ones that act upon the mind with the most profound and central force. All the other forms of worry can have something done about them. But the most drilling form of worry is driven down and down by the inevitable, and by the irrevocable. Its subject-matter is out of our control. The whirling edge of this worry is concentrated in its attack. Its sweep is narrow, its line is firmly cut. We cannot blunt its hard sharp edge with our fingers, or with anything else except Time. But we can pay keen attention to the spiritual geological strata into which it drills, and discover from it many values unknown on the superficial crust of experience. Rare jewels have been brought up out of the darkness for the glory of mankind by souls who have gone down very low into the black pit.

No emphasis upon the good uses of worry should be allowed to minimize its distress. Neither should it suggest that our worry-quota should be increased.

This entire discussion applies only to those moments when one finds oneself already in the midst of what the old New Englanders concisely call 'a tew.' Not by any means should worry be recommended to the rare person who has never tried it. He would only bungle it, and spoil the integrity of his own engaging type. He has a compensating specialty of his own. He is good at recovering from heedless mishaps, and he is able to survey his own wreckage with buoyancy and cheer. There may be times, to be sure, when his relatives feel that they would have to worry less if he would worry more. Physicians tell us that in fixed groups where one of the partners is extraordinarily relaxed and care-free, some other partner is likely to have a blood-pressure that is dangerously high. But there is no sense in trying to disturb the peace of the ever-merry optimist. We can only hope to harness to some good purpose the apoplexy of his friends.

The tension certainly is reduced if we know that worry, when it overtakes us, can be turned to power. At least, that fact is more helpful than most of the usual panaceas. Perhaps there are individuals who take comfort in the thought that others are worse afflicted, but that idea is only one more Vicarious Worry to the really generous heart. Besides, on account of the unduplicated twists of the individual spirit, every soul is peculiar and exclusive in its troubles. We are not helped by any glib pretense that our especial anxiety is a standardized or threadbare thing. The Children of Israel do not like to have the Moslems use their Wailing Wall.

It does us no good either, to be told smugly that if we will just expect them to, things will all come out right of themselves. From bitter experience we know that unless somebody bestirs himself, things probably will not. If we belong to the creative or reconstructive type, we must by nature pay heedful attention to predicaments, no matter how much we might prefer to travel easefully through life on the Shut-Eye train. When we

know that we are using all our best resources (including worry) intelligently,
then and only then will great religion help
us, and great music, and a walk in star-
light on a hill.

In the meantime, with the happiness
of others dependent on our actions, it is
the sheerest nonsense to tell us that we
never ought to worry. There are moments
when, all slang to the contrary notwith-
standing, we really *should*.

F. L. W.

RESTING UNCOMFORTABLY

AN ACQUAINTANCE of mine recently went part way through the top of his touring car and return, breaking the upper half of his leg, a few unimportant chips out of his skull, and shattering the bridge of his nose with unshatterable glass. His nurse, thinking to please him, read him the newspaper account of his accident, which closed with the words, 'Mr. Pettis is in Saint Joseph's Hospital, and is resting comfortably.'

Mr. Pettis, upon receipt of this news, snapped suddenly out of his morphine doze, and began at once to rip off his johnny, preparing to tear into the editor — skull, femur and all — and shouting at the top of his lungs, 'I'm *not* resting! And I'm *not* comfortable!' He was finally quieted by his own special nurse, two General Dutys, and another hypo. In other words, he didn't like it.

Mr. Pettis may or may not have been aware that according to all psychological standards he should have liked it. The psychiatrists and men of letters have gone berserk in telling us exactly what to say to the sick and injured. Of late they have enlarged the field to include the sad, the bereaved, and the aged. They instruct us to 'talk of something else,' and to 'bring in some outside interests.' Under no circumstances may you tell a sick person that he looks sick, or that you consider his plight in any way serious.

Now, we should be interested in a show of hands if any of the brothers honestly feel that they have been 'helped' by being told that they are getting better when they know they are getting worse, that they are looking just fine when they know they are looking terrible, or that their operation or accident was not serious when they know it was.

If one is really interested in the technique of giving pleasure to a patient (and why else should anybody wish to visit one) he may remember first that the sweetest word in all the world to a sick person is 'you.' (Or *vous*, or *tu*, or *du*, as the case may be.) The second most delightful word, of course, is 'your.' (Or *votre*, or *ton*, — or *dein*.) With these two words to work with, one may build up a fine afternoon for an invalid.

One of the most fortunate openings I ever heard was made by a sincere soul who boomed into the room next my friend Pettis, with, 'B'gosh, old boy, you certainly do look bleached out!'

Pettis and I could hear the 'old boy' having a glorious time all afternoon in his bleached out condition, with this perfect friend.

Really, there are very few pleasures that a sick man can enjoy — and two of these are the knowledge that his friends are sorry that he is laid low, and the knowledge that he has the reputation of bearing his troubles nobly. These thoughts can crowd out, at times, the more morose ones of expense, pain, loss of work, boredom, wife and child. And these two pleasures a caller can give him.

Tell the patient that everyone is inquiring about him, and tell him who. There is the grand old story of how you went into the bank and they all inquired. The cashier said that head-injuries are very painful. The janitor said that his wife cried all the morning the day she heard of the accident, and the President himself said he was glad your friend didn't die, because it would have been such a loss to the community. A patient will not die any sooner just because a Bank President is glad he didn't.

Aside from anecdotes of this kind, a caller may well limit his conversation to the responsive part of a Responsive Reading. Let the note be struck by the patient himself, and not by you walking about on two feet. If he tells you that he has had fifty-two stitches, say some short word like *gracious*. Or, if you disapprove of 'gracious,' say, 'My word!' or, 'You don't mean it! Fifty-two!' Come to think of it, you wouldn't like fifty-two stitches yourself, so why not concede it to be a large number and have done?

Then there is that little matter of luck. Perhaps it is just as well not to tell a patient that he is lucky. A person is lucky if he slips on a fruit-skin and rights himself without injury, but he is not especially lucky if he falls down stairs and breaks his neck, although he fails in the process actually to die. Therefore, do not tell an engineer that he is lucky that the open switch did not completely finish him off, unless you first explain that you mean 'lucky' in the sense that we are all lucky that loose tigers do not jump out of the shuttle-train and eat us all up — furs, feathers, and fingernails, complete.

You are lucky if your eyeglasses start to crash on the marble floor of the post-office, and a passing youth executes several figure eights and catches them in mid-air by their black ribbon. But the word 'luck' does not have exactly the fine shade of meaning to describe any kind of surgical operation, organic disease, or accident. At least, such delicate phases of these circumstances as are lucky, let the patient be the first to mention.

It is restful to think of the Oriental nations — notorious for their freedom from neurotic disease — inquiring with elaborate diplomacy of the afflicted, 'How is your honorable and unprecedented Rheumatism today, of whose terrifying quality I am not worthy to speak? In your place, my inferior bravery would be as nothing beside your stupendous and venerable Fortitude.' This gives a patient a cozy feeling that both his Rheumatism and his Fortitude are being appreciated, and he is inspired to keep on being brave.

The American plan, on the other hand, is to listen to the patient's symptoms (or not) and to respond cheerfully, 'Oh, well, walk a couple of miles, and forget it.' The only possible mental reaction to this advice is, 'How I do wish *you* had the rheumatism if you like it so well — you and your miles!' or some equally sweet Presbyterian thought.

Indeed, certain remarks to invalids are

calculated to elicit certain invariable replies. Take the motorcycle man in Number 14, who wakes up to find himself in a plaster cast, and say to him bracingly, 'But cheer up! You'll be out of it in three months.' He can only say dubiously, 'Still, three months is three months.'

The little kid had it right when the visiting minister said to her, 'But your cold isn't so *very* bad.'

'Doe,' replied the miserable little creature with dignity, 'but *I* should have bidd the wudd to say that.'

So she should. In fact, a patient is quite likely to be the 'wudd' to make light of his own affliction if he is given half a chance. Out of a clear sky say to your friend, 'Man! What an optimist! In your place, I'd be grousing.' Instead of starting in forthwith to grouse and to retro-grouse, the sick man will be likely to become more and more of an optimist, since courage to all men is a cardinal virtue.

If, then, you can succeed in giving

133

your friend a regular Olympic Field Day of appreciation, letting him choose all the games, and giving him the pleasure of knowing that in the face of such tribulation you consider him quite wonderful, you may not work signs and wonders with his knitting bone, but at least you will leave him resting — though uncomfortably — on his laurels.

G. C. W.

HUNTING ACORNS

WHEN a guest of mine, aged ten, told me that he had a large collection of acorns from various historic shrines, and that he would like to find a nice specimen in Washington to add to the collection, I beamed at him with the eye of the gratified Washington hostess, and promised him acorns by the peck.

The Capital City, it will be remembered, is lined with oaks. The oak is to Washington what the elm is to New Haven, the horse-chestnut to Paris, the linden to Berlin, the palm to Miami, the pine to Maine.

'But,' said my guest with a note of warning, 'we may not find any. There aren't any acorns at home this fall.'

Well, thought I, it would be different down here. I had always loved the sight of them ever since childhood days when we made them into dolls' teapots, and I knew just where the best ones could be found. Here was my chance to put this knowledge to good use.

On our first day of sight-seeing, we went cruising down the Potomac for a visit to Mount Vernon. We walked up from the boatlanding through the stately oak grove along the winding road; and on our way down we chose the narrow footpath which is fairly jostled out of its course by the trunks of oaks. We went up slowly and we came down slowly, and everywhere we searched.

'Hunting for acorns, son?' asked the attendant who had just been up to ring the warning bell for the boat. 'Nobody seems to find any this year. Never knew them to be so sca'se. But here's a big black walnut that will make a souvenir.'

My guest thanked the attendant and politely accepted the black walnut. But if you are a collector of rare coins, a gold medal is no substitute. If you are a collector of acorns, even the most magnificent black walnut will not do.

'Never mind,' said I confidently, as we went back on board the boat. 'I know a

136

place in Rock Creek Park where they are always thick.'

We went there the next morning, along the bridle path in the woods near Old Pierce Mill. No luck. We saw any number of last year's broken cups and weather-beaten hulls, but fossil remains were not what we had set our hearts on. Both of us were connoisseurs, and to suit us an acorn had to be this year's model, with a complete cup-and-nut formation, solid as a darning egg. A good sound specimen, I was told, will take on a beautiful permanent gleaming polish, if you hand-rub it with diligence and plenty of Old English Wax.

Therefore, at every historic landmark, we explored the premises eagerly with pointed sticks. We left no leaf unturned. We went carefully over Lafayette Park, and the Zoo, and around the Freer Gallery, and from the Corcoran to the Pan American, and behind the Library of Congress, and all over the Sylvan Theatre near the Monument, and around the Smithsonian, and down by the lagoon.

Wherever we walked along the streets
of Washington, we paused at every oak
tree, much as festive spirits in the old
days used to stop at every bar. People
thought that we were looking for lost
money or wrist-watches, and offered help.

We began to think that we had looked
for acorns so steadily that we were unable to see them; perhaps we were 'too
near the subject,' as our artist friends
would say. So we went for a long ride,
only getting out now and then to search
a little with fresh eyes. We looked along
the canal, and at Great Falls, and at
Wide Water, and in Arlington, and near
the Anglers' Club, and down on Con-
duit Road.

By this time it had dawned on us that
this was no year for acorns. Later it
came out in the newspapers that the
famine was unprecedented, and the public was urged to give a small fund toward
feeding the squirrels in the parks. But
it did seem to us that there must be just
one chance specimen in the whole of
Washington. This visit was supposed

to be highly educational; and topo-
graphically I feel sure it was. We had
gone so far on our search, however, that
at each new historic shrine we could not
help thinking of our quest: Admiral
Farragut; Oh, yes, here he is; but what
about acorns? Will they be here, yes or no.

At the very end of the visit, I decided
that my guest should at least have a
memento of our search to take home with
him, and I showed him how to make a
watch-fob out of beaten copper with an
acorn-and-twig design. Then, to get the
nitric acid quickly out of harm's way, we
took it into the woods to an old seques-
tered Dump. There we dug a hole, poured
in the rest of the acid, turfed the place
well over, and strewed it with tin cans.
And as we arose from our knees after
burying the last traces of our hopes,
what should we see on the hill beside us?
Great oak trees, and under the oaks,
acorns and acorns, lustrous, well-turned,
sleek brown shapes with pointed noses
and stout caps ruggedly embossed; acorns
as glossy as horse-chestnuts, and as firm

as Heart of Oak. They would polish like a sideboard and last till crack of doom.

We filled our pockets, and we heaped a battered tin quart measure from the Dump. We were happy as the sons and daughters of men are not very often happy.

And as we strode homeward along Connecticut Avenue, tin quart measure in hand, I reasoned within myself, saying, Is it not ever thus? Although we behold the Capitals of the world and the glories thereof, do we not every one of us pursue our acorns? Did not I once raise heaven and earth for a certain etching of a gargoyle that I wanted, in the very shadow of Notre Dame? I was discussing this topic later with a traveled friend, and she told me that certain of her chief regrets in life might be entitled, 'Acorns I have left behind me.' One of her acorns, she said, was a plaid Scotch blanket that she did not buy in Glasgow. And when she mentioned that, I remembered a damask tablecloth with rose-and-thistle pattern that I did not buy in

140

Brussels, and a squatty little pewter pitcher with a cover, of the variety called a 'tappithen,' that I did not collect in Warwick; and I remembered how I had hurried my mother-in-law across a London Bridge at twilight and away from a tempting window where slippers with a fur border were displayed in a sale of Oddments. I told her we had no time to lose, and that the exchange would be better in Paris, and she agreed. But in Paris we found no such cozy slippers with fur-lined edges and quaint toes. They were a typical pair of acorns, those London slippers, and in my remorseful imagination I can see them still.

In fact, some winter evening, I think that I shall give a candlelight party for some of our friends, and ask them to tell us about Acorns they have sought for vainly, or Acorns they have found and cherished, or Acorns they have given up looking for and discovered unexpectedly, or, most lamentable of all — the ones that they have found, and left behind.

F. L. W.

TRAVELING ALONE

SOME people can afford to travel. Others cannot afford to travel. And still others cannot afford *not* to travel.

Among the last-named class are principally the seekers after business, or rest, or health; those who wish to get warm, to get cool, to reach high altitudes or low, and those who frankly set out to seek a fortune. And a good way in which to seek any one of these things is to seek it alone.

It is possible, of course, to hunt in packs, and without doubt all genuinely timid persons and those who really wish to be alone should follow this method. Two or more persons traveling together appear to be so self-sufficient that strangers fear that their friendly advances may be unwelcome. Then too, some strangers are also timid.

A solitary traveler, on the other hand, will be noticed by fellow-travelers, befriended, advised, smiled at, and perhaps royally entertained. I offer this as a traveler who has tried both ways.

My own traveling has been actuated mainly by a modest desire to breathe during the months of August and September, and I started out one Fall to find a ragweedless little Island in Canadian waters. When I left the train at Eastport, I was so delighted to find that I was breathing without effort, through my nose, that I rode, still breathing madly, down the main street of Eastport for about a mile to the wharf, leaving my trunk sitting on the station platform. Completely carried away by the joys of my simple pastime, I got on the boat and watched the trunks come aboard, one by one. I suppose the sight of these trunks called my own to mind. Instantly, my New England anxiety rose to the ascendant, and in a frenzy of apprehension I told my troubles to the Cap'n of the boat.

'Have you got a check, Miss?' asked the Cap'n, supposing, I imagine, that I had probably lost that too.

143

Yes, I had my check and I showed it to him feverishly.

'Joe!' called the Cap'n, looking like a Rodin statue of Peace. 'Get the lady's trunk.' He tossed over my check. Checks never fall into the water when tossed by New Brunswick Cap'ns.

'Aye, aye!' said Joe, ambling off with my check to the telephone. He telephoned from some mysterious instrument on the pier to a taxi-man. The taxi-man appeared, got the check, taxied the mile to the Eastport station, secured the trunk and returned to the boat. That cost twenty-five cents. Meanwhile the boat waited, serene and unhurried. We started when everyone was ready to start.

In keeping with this incident is a grain of what I believe to be the truth about the technique of travel. Running through all the various and sometimes unpleasant experiences we find that stunning scarlet thread which we call Kindness of People. We may prove by wandering around that the general run of humanity is kind. It is kind especially to the sick and un-

144

fortunate, the poor, the injured, and the lonely; — in fact to those who need it most, the compassion and charity of men flows most surely. We also occasionally meet the traveler who should be boiled in oil, but it is usually possible to call the attention of heaven piously to his sad case, and keep out of his way.

A person alone frequently has the experience of eating each separate meal of the day with different tablemates. A technique for this situation which has stood the test of some little time, has given me one of the major pleasures of life — that of making a new friend. When a stranger is shown to my hotel table I glance up, smile, and say 'Good morning.' The responses are fascinating to observe. It is incredible to note how many interesting varieties of Good morning there may be. No matter what reply I may receive to this overture, I wait about two minutes and then ask, 'Are you staying long?' Sometimes the answer to the question is 'No,' without qualification, and in that case I make no more advances, but attend strictly to my dinner, although still in a receptive frame of mind. But the travelers who confine their conversation to 'Good morning' and 'No' are few and far between. And in the rest of the traveling population lies the real value of going away from home.

Many times I have thought how nearly I missed knowing a great naturalist simply because I had an evening appointment. But I took time to go through my invariable experimental questions, and discovered a new acquaintance who could tell me the name of the little sea-pigeon from description. It must not be understood that the naturalist began right off by telling me that he was a naturalist, or the dry-point etcher that he was dry-point, or the distinguished tenor that he was a distinguished tenor. But an expert in almost any line will be so much interested in his vocation that the subject will in time come to the surface.

Meeting so many people who are themselves traveling through a region should not mean that there is no time to get acquainted with the people who live there. Some regions fire us with energy, and others let our ragged nerves rest for a season. Among the real maritime Canadians you find yourself living by the tide rather than by the clock. And when a man lives by jags of time, each six hours long, he forgets to hurry. They do us good, these placid, courteous, and unhurried fishermen. They have a peculiar habit which I have not been able to fathom; that of apparent inability to answer a direct question. I spent five weeks trying to find out whether a herring were a grown-up sardine or not. I cannot remember how they ever evaded a direct answer, but some other replies I took down.

'When will Allingham's store open?' I asked, trying the door.

'Allingham's to Eastport, in his launch,' a man told me politely.

'When is the boat due?' asked a careless lounger from Boston.

'I ain't heerd her blow,' is the answer to that.

'When will it be high tide today?' I once heard a young woman ask — really, for swimming purposes, wanting to know.

'She ain't turned yet, lady,' replied the fisherman, taking off his cap, as if to the tide.

It isn't as if he didn't know the exact moment of high tide, either, for he lives by it. He fishes for one kind of fish at high tide, and for another 'on the turn.' But he won't tell.

It will be noted that all these questions have to do with the word *When*, and that is the very word which the tide makes you forget. They will help you into a boat, these kindly men, with a manner that a New York subway guard ought to see just once. If it is high tide, they walk helpfully beside you across the gangplank to the boat's hold; at low tide, they usher you to the boat's roof and steady you down a 'larder' to go below. For here the tides are twenty-eight feet high. The 'BayofFundy' has always been a piece of water apparently included in the joggraphy to bother the adolescent American

148

child who thinks till he sees it that a tide is a purely horizontal thing. But seeing that Bay, or in fact any Bay, or any other place, is the only real way in which to learn geography. It is impossible to forget the 'BayofFundy' if you have once crossed its 'rips' in summer and tried to imagine what these strange tides must mean in winter storms to those brave fishermen off the Grand Banks.

A danger which even the most innocent are likely to encounter is that of assuming that a fisherman knows nothing but fish or that a weir-tender knows nothing but weirs. Who would expect to find an artist photographer as proprietor of a hardware store — a proprietor who has given up keeping wool yarn for knitting sweaters because, as he says, what is the use if he sells it all the minute he gets it? But this is just the sort of thing one *should* expect.

We went into his store to buy a camera film, which he sold to us and offered to install. As his deft fingers worked like lightning over this installation, he shoved toward us with his elbow a pile of soft

Japanesey prints worthy of Hokusai himself.

'If you want to get some pretty pictures,' he observed apologetically, 'go out here to Digediguash.'

'Ah!' breathed my companion. 'Is it too far to walk?'

'No, a little better than a mile. *But* you'll have to cross the railrudd. And *look out for the train.* She comes by every day at two minutes before eleven.'

As my friend had spent a long and useful life in Brooklyn, New York, she at once assumed all responsibility of piloting me across the tracks at some odd moment of the day other than two minutes before eleven.

If one stays long enough in a locality, the very dogs take on individual personalities from which it is sad to part. Dumpling Mallory will follow you fishing but not walking. The Thompson spaniel will follow you to the Post Office, but never to church. Yo Fei, Florence Ayscough's Chinese dog, will follow you nowhere.

Roxy Kennedy, a beautiful blind setter,

always attends the movies, arriving late, and passes slowly under the knees of all present until he locates his family. Now if one is a stranger and does not even realize what Roxy's name is, or that he is *at* the movies, this is a novel sensation indeed. In fact, when I first experienced it, and my kindly neighbor whispered to me, 'It's only Roxy!' I cannot say that I felt reassured to any great degree.

However, it should surprise no traveler to meet the real Roxy himself, even at the movies. A novice at traveling is delighted and awe-struck when he meets even a friend's friend when far from home. The seasoned wanderer *expects* to know indirectly every third person he meets. He counts them off tranquilly: eeney, meeney, miney, mo. He thoroughly expects to recognize 'miney.' And then he says to Miney — eagerly or wearily, according to his type — 'Isn't the world small!'

It is, and it isn't. It is small enough for the orbits of all our friends to cross each other at some point, and plenty large enough for us all to start new orbits at any time at the slightest excuse. We may almost wish to stay the hand of science, which is fast bringing us pictures of our friends as they talk to us from Europe, which is air-conditioning our very houses around us, and inventing new serums to cure us and keep us at home.

But just as long as there are wheels, and sails, and wings left in the world; just as long as things like life, and change, and death remain — there will always be men in search of high adventure, traveling alone.

G. C. W.

PICNICS

HAVEN'T you ever been on a picnic?' we once asked a little Down East boy who was watching us open our baskets at sunset in a balsam grove.

'My mother she let me take my supper out in the yard once,' said he, 'but I ain't never been on no *rusticators'* picnic.'

We were so glad to find that summer visitors were still called 'rusticators' in that region that we invited him to supper on the spot.

To enjoy a picnic as it is capable of being enjoyed, a person should have something of the rusticator in his blood. His nature must be just remote enough from the rural to appreciate it, yet not so brittle with civilization as to be made miserable by it. He should have a relish for favorite landscapes, for choice companions, and for lunch. The lunch may vary from one mountaineer's invariable ration of 'one pound nut-bread, one pound cheese,' to

Christopher Morley's ample menu, which included among many other things doughnuts, 'calculated on the basis of three to each adult,' and inside each doughnut a neatly packed hard-boiled egg. The choice is unlimited, for the picnic is a stiff old world's most casual invention for the exercise of original taste.

Yet there are large numbers of very excellent and very gifted men who cannot abide a picnic. We know exactly how one of them can act on such occasions, for on our family picnics we always had a Problem Father along. He was lured thither by the known prospect of rare foods, but would have liked them far better at home. He took a camp-chair to sit on, and he encouraged his children to pursue watersports and field study as much as possible out of ear-shot, measuring our distance by as many light-years as we found convenient away from him.

He felt almost as strongly about the insects. And he was not alone in this. The most ardent field-and-stream enthusiasts I ever saw have a certain stated ritual that

they call 'disemgrasshoppering' one another at intervals as they walk. When you
are about to re-enter civilization on re-
turning from a day with them in the open,
one of them will ask politely, 'May I dis-
emgrasshopper you?' and you submit
yourself thankfully to careful search.
Even Mr. Harvey Gaul, in a moment of
complete disenchantment when he had
been taken out on one too many picnics,
once wrote morosely that he would bet his
last lily cup that all his wife's relatives
were ant-eaters.

Nobody really likes the ants. And
therefore it may be pleasant to recall two
or three picnics where there were none.

The first took place in a boat. There was
a guest in our town who had read John
Burroughs' account of how he watched
a whole lakeful of white pond-lilies opening in the morning as the sun's rays stole
gradually from flower to flower. She
wanted very much to see this lovely sight.
As it happened, our grandfather owned a
woodlot where there was a lily pond, near
the homestead where his own father used

to live. Our grandfather and our uncle had
supplemented the native lilies with roots
of lotus and Irish Loch Lily, and the
Helen Fowler, and the sturdy pink Mrs.
Richmond — that hardy creature that
puts forth buds till after frost, and sometimes sends up blossoms through a skim of
ice. We knew that between the cultivated
lilies and the wild ones, there would surely
be some ready to open. So we borrowed
the key to the boat, got up early on a
dewy Sunday morning, packed a thermos
kit with hot chocolate, took along some
fruit and cream and berries, woke up our
guest, drove out with her into the country,
and found our lake just emerging from a
trail of mist. Everything was so wet that
we had to dry off the thwarts of the boat
with sponges, and arrange a steamer-rug
in the stern as a place for our guest to sit.
While we were working, a light breeze was
clearing the open water, but the shallow
edges of the pond, where we were going to
find the water-lilies, were still hidden in
drifting shreds of mist. We could take our
time as we trimmed our craft, stowed our

provisions, unlocked the padlock, un-chained the boat, and shoved off.

That old lily-picking scow had been made to order years ago according to specifications invented by our grandfather, who designed it so that half a dozen little boys and girls could rush to one side of it and lean over to look at a fish, without disturbing its balance in the least. Our grandfather wanted us all to have the pleasure of catching his fish and picking his pond-lilies, but he did not want to have to dredge his pond for grandchildren. The scow was therefore much more like a diving-platform than a boat, and as we pushed off with our guest we proceeded through the water at the stately tempo of a royal barge. Even the cream in our cream-bottle rode sedately. We had the curious sensation that we were stalking the pond-lilies in the mist. We caught ourselves talking in whispers, and trying not to swish our boat against the rushes, as if we were afraid the lilies would take fright and refuse to open if we made any noise.

Perhaps on account of the coolness and
wetness left by the mist, it took a little
longer for the miracle to happen than Mr.
John Burroughs had led us to expect.
We drank our hot chocolate and ate straw-
berries and gazed about us to kill time.
Cat-tail shadows are exquisite at sunrise,
and so is dew on lily-pads, and so is the re-
flection of water-arum and pickerel weed
by a marshy shore. We sat so still that the
javelin-shaped reflections of the arrow-
head leaves at the edge of a little island
within an oar's length of us hardly stirred.
A row of turtles sat on a log beside us, a
scalloping row of glistening old shellbacks
with gleaming yellow spots, and they were
quiet too. And presently one of us noticed
that out in the cove a large bud with a
splash of sun directly on it was almost
open. We paddled out until the boat
swung up alongside it, and we could look
straight down into the incredible golden
heart of that snow-white opening flower.

In spite of our attentiveness from this
point onward, I do not think we could
honestly say that we watched any indi-

vidual water-lily go through the complete change from tight bud to fully opened bloom. The process was so gradual that the eye would stray; and there were too many new buds, including some rare pink ones, starting to open and needing to be pointed out and paddled toward for us to devote our gaze to one alone. Later it occurred to us that our lilies might have been uncommonly slow on that cool morning, and we asked a professional aquatic gardener if the blossoms ever open more suddenly than the ones we saw.

'Oh, no,' he said. 'They never do *pop* open. It's so slow, it would be quite a stunt to see them do it. After the sun strikes the water, it always takes 'em from twenty minutes to half an hour.'

There are few things more fragrant than pond-lilies freshly open in the early morning, and there is nothing more cool to feel of than their long wet stems. We gathered a few choice blossoms with their lily-pad leaves to float in low green bowls on certain Sunday dinner tables, and we turned our boat toward shore. Another

159

time, we said, we would concentrate on a single bud and keep a gimlet eye patiently upon it to the point of hypnotism if necessary, and catch all its slightest intermediary changes, like a slow-motion camera lens.

Another time, perhaps we may. But as it is, I am glad of that complete memory of mist and snowy water-lilies and pure fragrance, when we watched the whole pond open to perfection, like a flower.

My next picnic took place on a sandy beach, with salt water on both sides. We were having a family clam-bake, with a barrel of clams and a barrel of sea-weed, and a hot fire on some big flat stones in the middle of pebbles and pure white sand.

At a clam-bake in our family, we are as elaborately subdivided in our functions as a family of bees. Throughout the generations, there is always one contingent that washes clams, another that fetches and carries clams, one expert who tends the fire and rakes the stones clean for the bake, another who sorts the seaweed and wets the burlap, another who melts the butter and buttles it through the meal, and at least one discriminating individual who spends his time judging clams.

The clique that washes clams is always made up of devotees who are going to eat them largely. But the person who judges them is never one who likes them. If your heart is filled with the genuine lyric love of clams, you cannot believe that there could be such a thing in the world as a defective clam. It takes an expert clam-detester to view any such collection of exquisite little white clams as our clam-man always dug for us, and expect to find a single tell-tale open shell. When I first went on our clam-bakes, the judging was always done by a certain great grand-uncle Elisha, who had married into the family from southern Illinois. He came with us from love of company, but with scant sympathy for our Rhode Island and Connecticut shell-fish ways. I can see him now in his characteristic judging posture, his lean frame bent over the clam-pile, one long hand in pocket and the other hand severely ready to pounce on any innocent little bivalve whose shell was so much as chipped.

Uncle Elisha has long since vanished from the clam-flats of this earth, but years after he had died I happened at one of our clam-bakes to look up from my hereditary task of washing clams, and was electrified to behold Uncle Elisha's identical expression and posture in one of his little great grandsons whom he had never seen. There was the same imperious gesture, the same responsible expression of concentrated dislike. The old clam-man, who had known the family longer than I had, observed it too and caught my eye. For professional reasons, that trusty clam-man had never liked our imported Illinois uncle very well. 'Be you a-noticin' what I'm a-noticin'?' asked he, confidentially indicating the little great grandson with his clam-fork. 'He certainly does put me in mind of Elishy!'

It should hastily be explained that there were, on our clam-bakes, plenty of other viands for anybody who did not like clams; but personally I never noticed what the other provisions were. To me, and to others like me, it always seemed like a sinful waste of opportunity not to stick exclusively to clams. None too often in a life-time does mortal spirit have free access to whole bushels of them, freshly dug, well scrubbed, and scrupulously selected, on a breezy shore.

The only other picnic that I happen to remember without ants was in the snow. We had thought that the snow was over, for there seemed to be a genuine spring thaw. All the world was sparkling and dripping, and icicles were breaking off and falling from the branches everywhere. It was Saturday noon — tempting weather for a picnic. Do you suppose, we asked each other, that the snowdrops we planted will be up in the woods? The only way to find out was to go and see. I poured some hot tomato soup into a thermos jug, made sandwiches of our Saturday noon salad, and we started out.

The woods where we had planted our snowdrops were in a South Jersey tract which had hardly been touched since the

163

first settlers honorably bought the land from the Indians — purchasing it not for tawdry beads and whiskey, but for valuable commodities, including '30 match coats, 30 kettles and one grate one, 200 pelts, 60 scissors, and 100 jewsharps.' Best of all, those hundred jewsharps. We were newcomers to this region, and in our explorations of these woods we liked to imagine those wild tribes of Leni Lenape Indians perfecting their technique upon these instruments. Did they use them for songs of love, or War songs? And did the Sachems practice on them, or was it a young brave's art? We heard no ghostly jewsharps in the woods that day, but the region was full of other haunting music, melting water and tinkling icicles, and the rush of wind in the pines.

We went along our favorite walk, retracing the path that we had taken on our bulb-planting excursion in the fall. This is an annual custom wherever we happen to be: one walk in the October woods with a pocketful of snowdrops and a trowel, and then when the springtime snow is melting, another walk along the same path to see if the flowers are up. Finding early snowdrops in your own garden is plenty good enough; but there is a slight touch of extra magic about finding them in the woods. You put them there yourself, to be sure, tucking them in as casually as a squirrel with an acorn; but you never get over the perennial astonishment of seeing the flowers look so much at home.

There they were, a colony of them up, and three of them open, at the edge of an almost melted patch of snow. One dainty little 'perceneige' had opened its white wings out perfectly flat, each wing shaped like the blade of a propeller for a fairy plane. The other two were hanging their heads down as they should, little wax models of idealized snow-drops with their clear-cut pale green stems and leaves. We sat on a fallen tree beside them and started our luncheon; whereupon a gray cloud came over and it began quietly but vigorously to snow. It was one of those early spring snowstorms with great composite flakes of the fluffy, clinging variety in which you can see all the exquisite star-crystals when they alight upon your coat. Anybody who ever drank large snowflakes in a cup of hot tomato bisque will remember that it makes quite a prankish Jack Frost variation from tomato *au crouton*. We finished our soup-course before it got entirely drifted in, and we left our miniature garden standing crisply, each snowdrop with a little tuft of feathery snowflakes on its head.

The out-of-door excursion is not guaranteed to be the most comfortable of joys. But if you like it at all, it is one of the most revealing. I owe it a good deal of respect, because some of the happiest marriages that I chance to know about were made on picnics. This does not mean that there is necessarily any correlation between durable companionship and love of the open country. But any two who enjoy that taste in common can keep a permanent freehold upon something that in itself has a great deal of stability. The strong tower of their friendship is based on a substantive foundation, nothing less than the whole untenanted part of the planet earth. This gives them something to fall back on, and something to spread themselves out in. No matter how besieged they may be, they are always able, with half a day of sunshine and high wind, to air out and renovate their whole soul's edifice, filling it with freshness and the clear beauty of a new season — and doing it in Nature's own best housekeeping tradition, from the ground, up.

F. L. W.

PALACES

ONE man's palace may be another man's prison. If your friend loves the peaceful waters of the Sound, don't drag him out to Montauk Point to see the big breakers. (Although between you and me, the big breakers are the thing.)

The palaces herein described are of two kinds. A palace may be the high moment of ecstasy in any vocation, avocation, or mania; it may be but a moment, but it must be high. Then again, a palace may be real.

Can you imagine building a real palace of real material, exactly as you wish, exactly where you wish, and filling it with the things you most desire? Once I saw one.

It was built on a high hill on the edge of a blue bay. It was three times as long as it was wide, a peculiar formation allowing its builder to look from all its rooms at the sea, that shrine at which she worshiped. The windows toward the sea were not cur-

tained but framed, because they were not
windows but pictures. Joe's Point was
the painting in the back pantry. Pier and
Boats was in the servants' dining-room,
Red Buoy and Shoals was in the Master's
room, and Island of Pink Rocks hung in
the library. As I glanced about the
library for the first time, I almost wished
never to leave, but to live there forever
and die in the walls. Straight to the lofty
ceiling ran the bookcases, equipped with
step-ladders of teak-wood. Books two
feet and a half tall were there, illustrated
with enormous colored pictures, each a
painting in itself.

On a platform with two steps stood the
piano, one end upflung, with a Grieg Sonata on the rack. As if this were not enough,
a violin lay slantwise across its open case,
and the builder of that palace picked up
the violin and played it for us, while we
sat in the great window overlooking the
bay.

The glass of that window was wider
than the spread of your two arms, and en-
closed in its black casing was the sea, lav-

169

ender-blue with brilliant purple shadows
and tips of white. An island of pink rock
lay far out on its hazy surface, and flying
toward us came a yacht — all sails to the
breeze. If we wished to go down and meet
it, we might, for it belonged to the owner
of the palace; its skipper was her skipper,
the pier was her pier, and every breeze
that blew across from Fundy might be her
breeze.

In another room, exquisite in its setting
of white jade, colossal vases, and ancient
images, was a collection of sea-birds' eggs,
lettered with this quotation: 'I think that,
if required on pain of death, to name instantly the most perfect thing in the universe, I should risk my fate on a bird's
egg.'

As I examined with awe the frail and
beautiful things, the aged caretaker said
to me confidentially, 'If you sh'd bust
them eggs, Miss, your name would be
Mud — it would so.'

And there you have it. With the abil-
ity to replace that collection a hundred
times over, the collector still retained for

the material objects of her childhood's gathering, that thrilling attitude which alone had made them priceless. The beautiful buffy egg of the Noddy Tern meant to her a blue day in the Bahamas at fourteen. The pear-shaped green egg of the Murre, so shaped to prevent its rolling off its nest of bare rock, called to her mind a picture of thousands of comical penguin-like birds, each sitting upright on a single egg.

Not a detail of this palace received a worldly or bored reaction from its builder. She possessed the attitude of the eager and the open-minded. That sort of person is always willing to learn from adversity, ready to find some new adventure in the commonplace, repulsing nothing whatever which may lead to information, and eager at all times to add to the sum of his knowledge, knowing that each bit of knowledge has, finally, its corresponding ecstasy. This attitude brushes over the gold of even a real palace with infinitely more precious material.

In fact, this palace business is largely a matter of the open mind; and it is somewhat rare. Not everyone is able to open his mind and prop it open.

There is something absolutely charming to a person of this type about inevitable catastrophe; not in the catastrophe itself, but in its inevitableness. If it is really inevitable, this is a comparatively simple situation which calls for no judgment. He finds himself in that uncomplicated position of having no possibility whatever of deciding to *change* his situation, but only as to what method he shall pursue in enduring it. Endurance is simpler than constant decision; mankind itself has called it 'simple endurance.'

Perhaps this open-minded individual has to lie on his back for three weeks with his foot in the air. Very well. What can he do about it? Not a thing. He can, however, decide just what end he shall assign to this experience. He regards it not as coercion, but as a *chance*; a chance to learn something which nobody else precisely knows. From it he thoroughly expects to learn details of treatment and human reaction which may help him later

172

to the greatest of life's many satisfactions — that of actually understanding another fellowman in difficulty. Learning, learning, — he faithfully observes stimulus and response in himself as well as in his nurses, doctors, family, and friends. Every detail, however unpleasant, contributes to his one fell purpose which he calls 'more and better conclusions.'

That philosophy has kept many an injured man's foot in the air; not simply *patiently* in the air, but inquiringly, hopefully, regally, and with profound design. At the end, he finds himself at least at the front gates of a palace — the gate-key in his hand.

But there are situations which may be recognized at once as not calling for simple endurance. Instead of lying down submissively under misfortune, it is sometimes more to the point to sit up and busily braid a whip of small cords. Rebellion and protest sometimes clear the air — but they call for judgment. Anyone planning to act rather than to endure, should be sure to plan.

A home-maker with an untarnished reputation for complete self-control once 'thought it all out,' and one day whirled on her family and threw her pocket-book across the room. Out fell a rain of small change, a bottle of aromatic ammonia for fainting strangers within her gates, a bunch of family keys, shopping lists, gold and silver pencils, and a card labeled, 'What to do if I died.'

This simple act of protest marked an era for that woman. Her family lived for months thereafter with the knowledge that if pressed too far, 'Mother might throw her pocket-book.' Nobody had ever dreamed before that that mother had any feelings of her own, or any limits to her endurance, and this new knowledge reorganized the family, and put its queen on her throne.

Of course this should not be construed as advocating a New Nation of Pocket-Book Throwers. But if you should find yourself being a bit too much of a worm for the public good — just turn. You may see a palace.

PALACES

I once overheard an old gentleman talking with his wife in a railroad dining-room. The white-haired patriarch was poring over a time-table, when he looked up suddenly and said with eagerness, 'Mary, I was wrong! I made a mistake!'

Now Mary can say 'I told you so,' but that's *all* she can say. Oh, what a lovely place that wise old man is in! He is in a palace. 'I was wrong! I was wrong!' It has such a joyful lilt to it; a proper place in which to spend many happy hours. 'I was wrong' is such a safe and comfortable palace that it seems strange that so many people prefer to march out of it with shield and buckler, shouting, 'I was right!'

Aside from situations that arise in daily life, we can make our way to known palaces by deliberately changing our geography. We all know where they are — for us. Some of us may trudge, stick in hand, for miles, to a violet covered hill. There, sitting on the dry, crumbling greenish-gray moss, now pulling with gentle tweaks the heavenly lavender flowers, now gazing across the valley at

175

the pastel-colored hills of Spring, we fill
our hands with violets and our souls with
hope.

We may go instead to the sea, or to the
lakes, or to church, or to the Symphony.
There is a time always in a 'good' Symphony, when the first violins playing together do not sound like one colossal
violin, but (for which God be praised!)
like many, many violins. The conductor
throws the sound away from him like a
fabric and then beckons it back. On and
off they go — now receding, now return-
ing. And under this huge canopy of sound,
the conductor begins to hurl darts at the
horns. Put on all your workmen, Dr.
Stokowski — your skilled artisans and
your silversmiths, your Tubal-Cain and
Jubal-Cain, and build for us a palace!

At the end, we find ourselves living in
a palace, just as we knew we would,
although we may be riding home in a
bus.

Then too, there are many places in the
world which do not advertise themselves
to be palaces at all, but quite the contrary.

I can see one of these with no effort at all; it is a hospital room rigged up with a fracture bed and pulleys, a great 'cradle' for the feet, an iron 'rainbow' arching over the whole — the complete panoply of pain. But that room was filled and crowded so full of grave sympathy, and tireless ministration, and expertness, wisdom, and devotion to duty, that they burst the ceiling and shot the roof up into many glistening spires.

Finally, there is nothing which can show a human soul just what palaces he does inhabit, so startlingly as a complete devastation of his material and physical possessions. A mere knowledge of the size of Betelgeuse will not help us then, but a thrilling sense of its glory may. Then is the time when our palaces stand out sharply against their background of nothing. They are all we have. That person is happy who has built all the palaces he could, and has recognized all those of sudden fairy origin which flashed into being of themselves and stood beside his path. His whole sky is full of flashing, cloud-capped pinnacles, some of gold, some of crystal, and some of granite.

He finds that he can live in them — for he *has* lived in them! And surely one who habitually moves in and out of palaces, whether of glass or gold, and finds himself to be sincerely at ease in all of them, must be at heart a prince — and possibly a king. To him, these shining palaces are Home.

G. C. W.

THE END